The **ANTIRACIST HEART**

ROXY MANNING, PhD and SARAH PEYTON

# THE ANTI RACIST HEART

## A SELF-COMPASSION AND ACTIVISM HANDBOOK

BK

Berrett–Koehler Publishers, Inc.

Berrett-Koehler Publishers, Inc.
1333 Broadway, Suite 1000
Oakland, CA 94612-1921
Tel: (510) 817-2277
Fax: (510) 817-2278
www.bkconnection.com

ORDERING INFORMATION

QUANTITY SALES. Special discounts are available on quantity purchases by corporations, associations, and others. For details, contact the "Special Sales Department" at the Berrett-Koehler address above.

INDIVIDUAL SALES. Berrett-Koehler publications are available through most bookstores. They can also be ordered directly from Berrett-Koehler: Tel: (800) 929-2929; Fax: (802) 864-7626; www.bkconnection.com.

ORDERS FOR COLLEGE TEXTBOOK / COURSE ADOPTION USE. Please contact Berrett-Koehler: Tel: (800) 929-2929; Fax: (802) 864-7626.

Distributed to the US trade and internationally by Penguin Random House Publisher Services.

Berrett-Koehler and the BK logo are registered trademarks of Berrett-Koehler Publishers, Inc.

Printed in the United States of America

Berrett-Koehler books are printed on long-lasting acid-free paper. When it is available, we choose paper that has been manufactured by environmentally responsible processes. These may include using trees grown in sustainable forests, incorporating recycled paper, minimizing chlorine in bleaching, or recycling the energy produced at the paper mill.

*Library of Congress Cataloging-in-Publication Data*
Names: Manning, Roxy, author. | Peyton, Sarah, 1962– author.
Title: The antiracist heart : a self-compassion and activism handbook / Roxy Manning, PhD, and Sarah Peyton.
Description: First edition. | Oakland, CA : Berrett-Koehler Publishers, [2023] | Includes bibliographical references and index.
Identifiers: LCCN 2023006168 (print) | LCCN 2023006169 (ebook) | ISBN 9781523003785 (paperback ; alk. paper) | ISBN 9781523003792 (pdf) | ISBN 9781523003808 (epub) | ISBN 9781523003815 (audio)
Subjects: LCSH: Antiracism. | Racism—Psychological aspects. | Discrimination—Psychological aspects. | Change (Psychology) | Social change.
Classification: LCC HT1563 .M236 2023 (print) | LCC HT1563 (ebook) | DDC 305.8—dc23/eng/20230331
LC record available at https://lccn.loc.gov/2023006168
LC ebook record available at https://lccn.loc.gov/2023006169

First Edition

31 30 29 28 27 26 25 24 23   |   10 9 8 7 6 5 4 3 2 1

Book producer and text designer: BookMatters
Cover designer: Susan Malikowski, DesignLeaf Studio
Cover illustration: Mireille van Bremen (The Visual Mediator) and Roxy Manning
Author Photo: Kathryn Krogstad

For all who risked everything,

advocating for change.

For all who laid a stone,

paving the path to Beloved Community.

For all who gave everything,

nurturing the next generation.

And for those to come,

you are our wildest dreams.

—*Roxy*

For everyone

who is exploring choosing love

with authenticity

and without backing down.

—*Sarah*

# CONTENTS

# ACTIVITIES

*Exercises to Release Contracts*

*Journaling Prompts*

## Questionnaires

## Worksheets

# FOREWORD

Systemic change is deeply personal. This simple but paradoxical idea is perhaps the key reason most efforts at systems transformation are so disappointing. Something in the very word "system" or "systemic" consistently leads us astray—seeking some magical change "out there" when the most intransigent aspects of the *"out there"* **are inseparable from our habits of thought and action** *"in here."*

> —MARY SCHEETZ, former assistant superintendent, Waters Foundation, and PETER SENGE, MIT Sloan School of Management and Society of Organizational Learning

*The Antiracist Heart: A Self-Compassion and Activism Handbook*, written by Roxy Manning, PhD, and Sarah Peyton, neuroscience educator extraordinaire, is a profound and immeasurable gift. These two dedicated social justice warriors offer guidance, wisdom, and practices that support both the individual and the collective need to revision and redesign how we address change. Given the morass of contemporary society, it is easy to succumb to the rampant individualism and dualistic thinking infused into Western culture. We often live disconnected lives prompted by identity formation, rationalizations, how we regard "others"—which often includes ourselves—along with

*Epigraph*: (emphasis added) Mary Scheetz and Peter Senge, "Systemic Change and Equity," ECCBN: Equity-Centered Capacity Building Network, https://capacitybuildingnetwork.org/article3/.

the deep internal and external systems of power, economics, and other social structures.

This is not just another book to read. It is to be studied and practiced. Intergenerational systems and historical suffering require mending. These systemic patterns take place inside our beings while informing the conscious and unconscious habits of mind, body, and emotion. They influence and drive how we make meaning of the worlds in which we live. Can we reimagine and reconstruct a future that acknowledges our interdependence, which is key to our survival? How do we build beloved communities? Neurobiology teaches that it is important to mend ourselves and society through gentleness, warmth, and understanding rather than harsh judgments and punishments.

Change work is difficult and inevitable. We need to expand our awareness along with a level of inquiry that is guided by deep curiosity. In masterful and transformative ways we as readers, rather than being absorbed into ever-changing explanations, analyses, and rationalizations, are invited into a deeper understanding of how our brains can effectively address traumas that permeate every level of the systems in which we move and have our ways of being. Scientifically, the neurobiological underpinnings of trauma and healing—including intergenerational trauma—provide key tools that the authors show us how to use for our individual and collective development. The handbook exercises invite us, the readers, to practice habits of mind in ways that build hope, wellness, and cohesion internally and externally. We are not only walking new pathways to change, we are also engaging in the power of transformative learning that allows us to truly activate love for ourselves, each other, and the planet.

—Shakti Butler, PhD, Founder and President Emerit
World Trust Educational Services, Inc.

# Introduction

## Where We Came from and Where We Invite You to Go

*From Roxy:*

I was born in Trinidad, a small island in the south of the Caribbean Sea. When my family emigrated to Harlem, New York, when I was seven, none of us anticipated what it would mean to enter a culture so explicitly affected by white supremacy culture (the attitudes, assumptions, and privileges that create a conscious and unconscious prioritization of people who are white) and the long-term effects of the institution of slavery. I struggled to make sense of the world and my place in it. Although my two-parent family was not wealthy in Trinidad, the impoverished community we moved to in the United States was very different from the one we left behind. Many of my new classmates didn't live with both their parents. In Trinidad we wore uniforms to school and were physically punished by our teachers for untidy clothing or dirty hands. In the United States I still wore freshly ironed skirts and blouses to school with ribbons in my hair. This marked me as different from my classmates, who wore jeans, clean or not. Every day at lunch time, my father picked my siblings and me up from school and brought us home, so that he could cook us a warm, healthy meal. My classmates sometimes went hungry.

When I was thirteen, six years after arriving in the United States,

I began attending school in the Upper East Side of Manhattan. My classmates were mostly white and Asian. It was the exact opposite experience of my schooling in Harlem. Many students had resources. They had money to buy lunches both on- and off-campus; they wore fashionable clothes (including the jeans my parents would never let me wear). Some students took after-school lessons, joined sports teams, and went away on vacations with their families. I didn't know how to make sense of the difference between these two groups of classmates. I didn't understand that what I had judged as deficits in my Harlem classmates and their families actually were constrained behaviors that resulted from generations of racist policies, ideologies, and practices. I did not understand the power of the white supremacy system and resulting beliefs that have endured for centuries, limiting the options for those in my Harlem community while expanding opportunities for families in my Upper East Side community. Without a framework of understanding, I unconsciously internalized racist perspectives.

Ibram X. Kendi defines racist ideas as "any idea that suggests one racial group is inferior or superior to another racial group in any way."[1] I certainly held those ideas. I believed what was being said in every book I read and every show I watched. I believed in this all-pervasive idea that each person was solely responsible for their own success or failure. I believed that community failure was a result of individual failure. This narrative left me with little compassion for the people in my home community. I remember looking around and thinking to myself, *If these Black Americans worked harder, if these parents cared more, if these kids had more pride in themselves—things would be different. Their suffering is their fault.*

This was a double-edged sword. In middle school when I began, for the first time in my life, to bring home C and B grades, I turned that lack of understanding and compassion on myself. *If I worked harder, if I tried more, if I wasn't lazy, then I would be doing better. My failures are my fault.* Just as I was unable to see the way centuries of racist policies had formed the two communities through which I moved, I was unable to see how those policies, and the ideas and behaviors they reinforced, impacted my capacity to thrive in a majority-white educational setting. I changed schools but still encountered the same racist ideas and behaviors in my new school. However, I also encountered people who were lifting up antiracist ideas. I met students and some teachers who did not accept the racist narratives that had guided my development thus far. Instead, they adopted what I would now recognize as a fierce antiracist stance. Kendi writes: "To be antiracist is to think nothing is behaviorally wrong or right—inferior or superior—with any of the racial groups. Whenever the antiracist sees individuals behaving positively or negatively, the antiracist sees exactly that: individuals behaving positively or negatively, not representatives of whole races.... Behavior is something humans do, not races do."[2]

I began the long journey toward recognizing that the behaviors and conditions I saw in my Harlem community were a response to the pervasive racism that touched every member of that community, not a sign of inferiority or lack of initiative in my Black peers. I began to recognize that the behaviors I hated in myself were not a sign that I was a flawed Black person, but a response to the gauntlet of racist ideas and behaviors I ran through each day. In learning that, I began to understand the importance of compassion. I had to learn how to acknowledge the horrors of racism and mourn its ongoing impact, because that is how I could find the energy and will to stand up against it.

As I began this work of self-compassion to free myself of the judgments and internalized racism that paralyzed me, one option that initially offered significant relief emerged. As I fought to reclaim my sense of my own value and capabilities, I began putting down white people whom I saw as racist. It was easy for me to look at white people with suspicion and to interpret any negative behavior not as a sign that the individual was doing something that was impacting me negatively, but as proof that white people were bad. Learning about Dr.

Martin Luther King Jr. and especially his emphasis on "The Beloved Community" showed me the trap into which I had fallen. As long as I judged some people or groups as irredeemable or worthless, I could not trust I would not be judged in the same way. As long as I placed myself and people like me in the group of people who were good, and white people and people with structural power in the group of those who were bad, I was buying into white supremacy thinking that asserted there are good people and bad people, good races and bad races. If I truly supported the values of Beloved Community, I needed to direct compassion not only to myself but also to those whose behavior I wanted to change.

This handbook aims to provide tools for people who share this vision. You can apply lessons in this handbook to other forms of privilege such as those related to gender, sexuality, religion, age, and so on.

*From Roxy and Sarah:*

Written by a Black and a white author, this handbook walks a difficult but important path. It is for two groups of people. The first group is the Global Majority. This is a collective term that refers to people who are Black, Arab, Asian, Brown, multiheritage, indigenous to North America or the Global South, and/or have been racialized as "ethnic minorities." Globally, these groups currently represent approximately 85 percent of the world's population, making them the global majority.[3] For simplicity, we call the second group "white"; this group includes people of European descent. Although the benefits accorded to whiteness are prevalent throughout the world, there are also cultures where people have inherited structural power—for example, a high-caste person in India. This handbook uses racism as a focal point for learning, but the lessons also apply to power or privilege due to caste, gender, sexuality, religion, age, and other categories. If you are a person within a high-privilege group—for instance, a high-caste person in India—consider how the dynamics that we discuss in relation to whiteness show up in your life and community.

In order to change the world, we need self-compassion. Our working definition of self-compassion is:

- to turn toward ourselves with warmth and understanding as much as possible, especially when things are hard and emotions or judgments are running high;

- to stand by and accompany ourselves through life's pain and misfortune, and through unbearable truths;

- to see the larger context of our lives and to see past our own and others' actions to our hearts;

- and to live with gentle care and include everyone, even ourselves, in Beloved Community.

Self-compassion is a core capacity that everyone can use in the work to dismantle white supremacy systems. This handbook is for folks from the Global Majority who are seeking strategies to uproot practices and beliefs that impair their capacity to move through the world grounded in a sense of connection with the whole community. It's for those who want to shake off shackles of win-lose, good-bad thinking that are emblematic of white supremacy ideology and reach for the possibility of a different world. This handbook will support those who want to feel more confident that they matter without requiring that others (regardless of group) matter less. It's for folks who want the power to stand in their fierce commitment to interrupt racist behavior and practices they encounter in a way that liberates their community while creating a world they want to pass on to the next generation, one in which all communities are free. This handbook is for people who recognize that we are all interdependent and that truly, as the great Fannie Lou Hamer said: "Nobody's free until everybody's free."[4]

This handbook is also for white people engaging in the work of antiracism, especially those who have found their inner voices harsh and unforgiving. It is for everyone who would like to bring about change with a life-supporting self-warmth instead of self-criticism. Sometimes white people who want to engage in antiracism work are stopped by harsh inner voices or by the harshness of the outer world. If people can live in an inner stream of nourishing self-compassion, they will persist in their antiracism work. This handbook helps to develop that self-compassion.

*From Sarah:*

My name is Sarah Peyton. I am white and didn't realize that whiteness had any meaning for the first fifty years of my life. Then, thanks to learning what we are sharing in this handbook, I discovered that all the bad things that had ever happened to me (trauma, domestic violence, low income, etc.) did not weigh enough to wipe out the societal advantages I can access because I am white. I had thought that because all those bad things happened to me, my whiteness didn't count. Those things *do* count, but they don't give me a pass on being a part of white supremacy culture and benefiting from systemic racism (the ways that white supremacy ideology becomes embedded in every aspect of society and culture). I actually have far more advantages than I want to have—or want to know that I have. The only way through my own resistance was to lean into self-compassion. As I started to understand the scale of harm that was being done through the adoption of white supremacy beliefs, I felt shame, because I also began to understand that since my body has white skin, I am a collective participant in that harm. There's no way forward from the pain of that realization except through self-compassion—without it, many white people just stop there, felled by the pain and shame, and don't move forward at all.

For as long as I can remember, my longing has been for Beloved Community, for a world where everyone can thrive and where there is a thoughtfulness for each person, who they are and what they need. I thought we had made progress toward that since the time of Martin Luther King Jr. When I learned about the persistence of systemic racism, I started to see the advantages I had not realized I had, including the advantage of not knowing that I was white. As long as I didn't know I was white, I didn't have to catch glimpses of my collective participation in the harm being done by systemic racism. As understanding dawned, I also felt bewildered. How could we not have made significant changes? How could it make sense that not everyone wanted a life of inclusiveness, that not everyone was reaching for it?

Since I love neuroscience, I turned to it to try to make sense of this conundrum. I knew that at birth, babies can tell all faces apart, no matter their ethnicity. What I didn't know was that by three months old, babies blur faces that are different from the faces of the baby's closest people, resulting in a favoring of the faces that are most like the ethnicity of the baby's closest circle.[5] This is the earliest beginning of the pattern-making that later leads our brains to normalize structural and systemic racism.

This kind of pattern-making was in my brain too, pushing me to discount people from the Global Majority. When I discovered that not only do I have systemic advantages, but that my brain is also unconsciously doing personal harm, I wasn't compassionate with myself—I was self-critical. I tried leaning into self-compassion, but I thought, *How could compassion help when my own brain is causing harm to other people?* I had contempt for myself for not knowing what was happening, and I had contempt for all human brains, including my own, that had power and privilege (since, as we will explore in this handbook, privilege decreases empathy and care for community). Only as I learned more deeply about the neuroscience behind racism, and about how the systems that we live in grind everyone down, was compassion able to come.

I learned that if what we want is Beloved Community and comprehensive change in our harmful social systems, what we need is compassion and self-compassion, every step of the way. Feeling self-contempt only leads to more belittling, impatience, and resentment. Although self-contempt feels like the right response to learning that I participate in harm, self-contempt actually perpetuates harm. Self-contempt is harm's secret weapon for retaining the patterns that separate us. As difficult as it may feel to find self-compassion and self-warmth, they are the foundation of meaningful change to the harmful social systems (and brain patternings, or conscious and unconscious beliefs) that we seek to alter.

Since white people have benefited so extraordinarily from systemic racism in lending, building wealth, education, legal immunity and protection, and professional advancement, to list just a few advantages, does this mean that white people are doomed to be racist? Thankfully, no. Everyone has the option of being antiracist instead of racist. But, as Kendi writes, it is impossible to be neutral and innocent in this system.[6] If people are not engaged, they are complicit. There is no middle ground in the struggle against racism: one is either actively confronting racial inequality or allowing it to exist through action or inaction. No matter what group we belong to, the more we learn about systemic racism and its harmful impacts and about the neuroscience of unconscious pattern-making, and the more we combine this knowledge with self-compassion and humility, the more choice we have about the patterns our brains follow. With more choice we gain leverage as activists, and we are better able to stay grounded and act in accordance with our intentions for the well-being of the world, even when we are in the middle of chaos and uncertainty.

*From Roxy:*

Over the decades I've been doing this work, people have asked me, "Where can I read your book?" However, for reasons you will understand if you read *How to Have Antiracist Conversations*, I had no book to offer.[7] Whenever I seriously imagined writing the book, all the old messages of not being good enough would surface, and I would drop the idea. After several years of working and learning from Sarah about the role that unconscious contracts we make to ourselves in order to stay safe play in our lives, I stumbled upon a deeply embedded contract that I had made to myself, one firmly grounded in racist ideas. It went: "I will keep myself safe by not writing anything substantive because I will become the target of racists and I will learn that I have nothing of value to share. I will refuse to write no matter the cost to myself."

Using the insights Sarah shares about how our brains respond to trauma, I was able to work with this contract and better hold myself and my fears with self-compassion. This practice made it clear that I wanted not just to bring my ideas into the world but to offer strategies to help people use them. I wanted to write this handbook with Sarah because I am convinced we are all more effective in our antiracism work when we combine practices for antiracist conversations with neuroscience tools. When we bring body-based practices that pay attention to cognitive patterns (and help us release fear and shame) into our antiracist conversations, we are more capable of integrating antiracism into our daily lives.

*From Sarah:*

When the opportunity came to co-create this handbook with Roxy, to further support her book *How to Have Antiracist Conversations*, I was stunned and grateful.[8] Roxy's dedication to working toward Beloved Community has become a touchstone of hope for me in this world. Combining her emphasis on practical skill-building for antiracism with the latest neuroscience research on bias and trauma lets us explore new ways of transforming human systems of social inequality.

*From Roxy and Sarah:*

In *How to Have Antiracist Conversations*, Roxy provides the theory and concepts that inform the Authentic Dialogue approach she has developed. Authentic Dialogue is an approach to difficult conversations

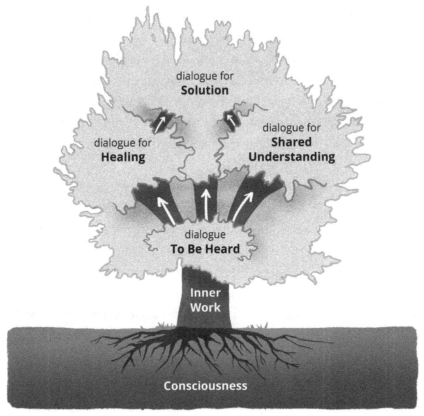

FIGURE 1. Map of Authentic Dialogue
© Mireille van Bremen and Roxy Manning

that flows from our commitment to the consciousness necessary to create Beloved Community through four dialogue options (Figure 1).

Readers of that book will gain a solid understanding of elements of Beloved Community, Nonviolent Communication, and the impacts of white supremacy culture in addition to learning and seeing modeling of the Authentic Dialogue process. In *The Antiracist Heart*, you will have opportunities to further explore those concepts through their application to your life and work. Journaling activities and questionnaires invite self-reflection while specific activities help you move from theory to practice. As you read this handbook, we encourage you to notice any places where it becomes difficult to persist due to guilt, shame, exhaustion, or helplessness. If the content becomes heavy for you in certain sections, remember that you can always skip ahead and do the exercises first and then return to the reading portions. The exercises are meant to help you absorb the material and to decrease feelings of shame, guilt, and helplessness, which will enable you to bring more fiercely compassionate and self-compassionate action to your antiracism.

A note about the structure of this handbook: Sections with the heading "Antiracism Concept" and the accompanying exercises are written by Roxy and therefore the use of "I" in those sections refer to Roxy. Similarly, sections with the heading "Neuroscience Concept" and the accompanying exercises are written by Sarah and the use of "I" in these sections refer to Sarah. Both Roxy and Sarah are Certified Trainers of Nonviolent Communication, a process formulated by Dr. Marshall B. Rosenberg. Principles of Nonviolent Communication, including a consciousness of interdependence and shared power, underlie the inner and outer dialogues throughout this handbook. Compassionate communication is supported by four components of Nonviolent Communication: observations (instead of evaluations), feelings (instead of thoughts), needs (instead of strategies), and re-quests (instead of demands). Roxy has expanded on these concepts in her Authentic Dialogue work, which lets Nonviolent Communication address systemic inequality, including racism, and Sarah integrates these components into the healing of trauma.

UNCONSCIOUS CONTRACTS
## Do-No-Harm Vows

As mentioned, a very effective tool for moving out of self-sabotage and self-limitation into action and self-compassion is the work with unconscious contracts. These are agreements we have made with ourselves, which we often don't know about, or the causes of which we are not aware of, that keep us bound into old ways of being, thinking, and reacting, so that we stop ourselves from expression, from compassion and self-compassion, and even from fully entering our relationships.

The unconscious contract that gets in most people's way when they are learning about systemic racism is the Do-No-Harm vow. It can make white folks unable to see what's happening, and it can make Global Majority folks unwilling to respond with fierce protectiveness. Do-No-Harm vows are essentially undoable in our present system, so they place anyone who has privilege in a double-bind. No one wants to do harm, but the way we live causes unavoidable harm: as white people in white supremacy culture, we harm the Global Majority; as humans, we harm the climate and the other species that live on this planet; if we are in the global north, we harm people with less access to resources. Instead of facing these harms, we often pretend that they do not exist, so that we can believe that we are keeping our promise to do no harm.

If you have a Do-No-Harm vow, it can be hard to read this handbook, because we see our collective responsibility for the harm of systemic racism. I, Sarah, promise, it does get easier once we release these unlivable contracts. Once we are able to have self-compassion and acknowledge the many ways we can impact others without intending to, we can reduce the amount of harm that we perpetuate because we can actually see what is happening. The problem with Do-No-Harm vows is not that they want to lessen harm (indeed, Buddhism contains a number of similar, life-affirming commitments), it is that they are too rigid and don't let us see the real and compromised system we live within.

 **QUESTIONNAIRE**
## Do I Have a Debilitating Do-No-Harm Vow?

If you are curious to discover whether you have a Do-No-Harm vow, you can explore these questions. Note that a "yes" answer to each

question leads to collapse, debilitating shame, or inaction. Give yourself one point for each "yes."

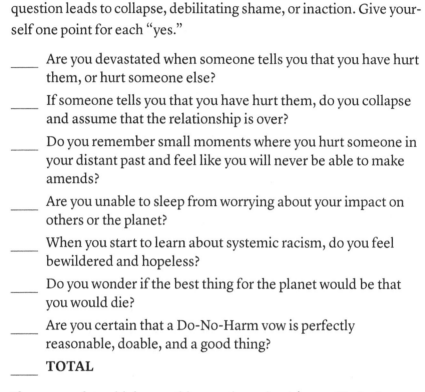

_____ Are you devastated when someone tells you that you have hurt
them, or hurt someone else?

_____ If someone tells you that you have hurt them, do you collapse
and assume that the relationship is over?

_____ Do you remember small moments where you hurt someone in
your distant past and feel like you will never be able to make
amends?

_____ Are you unable to sleep from worrying about your impact on
others or the planet?

_____ When you start to learn about systemic racism, do you feel
bewildered and hopeless?

_____ Do you wonder if the best thing for the planet would be that
you would die?

_____ Are you certain that a Do-No-Harm vow is perfectly
reasonable, doable, and a good thing?

_____ **TOTAL**

If you scored 4 or higher on this questionnaire, it's very likely that you
have one or several unconscious Do-No-Harm vows.

We can make many such contracts, and they can be personal or
global. A personal contract benefits me or a parent. A global contract
benefits the world. An example of a personal Do-No-Harm vow is: "I
promise myself that I will never be inattentive or distracted, in order
to stop my mother from being disappointed in me, no matter the cost
to myself." This isn't livable since everyone is always sometimes inattentive. But whenever I'm inattentive, the cost is that I have horrible
shame and expect people to be disappointed in me.

These contracts rule us if we do not know that they are in effect.
The way we release ourselves from these contracts is to make them
explicit and to ask ourselves if we still want them, even at such a cost.
I can release a contract that benefits me or a parent, and I can invite

myself to do something livable instead. For example: "Oh, Sarah, that isn't doable. I release you from this contract, and instead I invite you to know that being inattentive is part of being human, and to know that you can circle back around to people and make repairs."

An example of a global Do-No-Harm vow is: "I promise that I will live without doing harm, in order to straighten out this messed-up world, no matter the cost to myself." If I discover that I have done harm, the cost might be that I will believe that I should not be alive. If my contract benefits the world, the world has to release me from my contract. I just check in with the world: "World, did you hear Sarah's vow?" I become the world for a moment, and I answer my own question, to see if the world has an invitation for Sarah. For example: "Sarah, sweetheart, that's a beautiful vow but not currently doable. I release you from this contract, and I invite you to straighten up whatever you can without doubting your aliveness."

We invite you to use the "General Worksheet to Release Unconscious Contracts" to make explicit and release unconscious contracts. Return to this worksheet throughout the handbook in response to various types of contracts that we make with ourselves. For Do-No-Harm vows I recommend trying this worksheet two ways: The first time through, try it with a personal reason for making the contract, like keeping yourself safe or making your mother happy. The second time through, try a global contract, like saving the world.

### GENERAL WORKSHEET
## to Release Unconscious Contracts

I, (YOUR NAME HERE), promise myself that I will:
*(What will you do or believe—in this first worksheet practice, try "do no harm.")*

_____

_____

_____

in order to:

*(To find your "in order to," say the words and then follow them where they go, capturing whatever you find arising.)*

---

---

---

no matter the cost to myself.

*(Write a few lines about what the cost of this vow is to you.)*

---

---

---

Now ask yourself, "Self (or world), did you hear this vow?"

☐ Yes ☐ No

*(If "no," simply read the vow aloud to yourself again.)*

Now ask yourself, "Self (or world), would you like to keep (or would you like the Self to keep) this vow, even though it has such a cost?"

☐ Yes ☐ No

*(If "yes," acknowledge any past trauma and any worries you have about not surviving that underlie your contract—"Yes, of course this promise makes sense, based on past experience"—and ask again. If you still want to keep the contract, put a star by it so that you can revisit it later in your reading.)*

*(If "no," you no longer want to keep the contract, complete the release and invitation as follows.)*

I, (YOUR NAME HERE), dissolve this contract and instead I invite myself to:

_____

_____

_____

With our Do-No-Harm vows no longer keeping us in delusion about the continual harm we exert as part of the collective, it becomes easier to practice new skills that allow us to differentiate between individual and systemic harm, and to bring fierce compassion and self-compassion to our antiracism work. In each chapter of this handbook, you will learn about systemic racism and the contracts we make with ourselves, explore relational neuroscience and how systemic racism affects brains, and find exercises that help you explore the relationship between personal history and societal structure. Combining the knowledge with the exercises helps to open the door to self-compassion and embodied understanding, which offers new possibilities for responding to difficult conversations and situations. Doing the practices in this handbook regularly (with no more than three weeks between each chapter) will lead to the most growth and nurturing of new brain matter.

Difficult material is often made more difficult by outdated agreements and contracts we have made with ourselves that help us to make sense of the world. For example, we could have agreements like "I will believe that I'm responsible for everything that is wrong," or "I will not take responsibility for anything." To make learning easier, most chapters provide a template for finding and releasing this type of agreement or contract that we have made with ourselves.

# 1

# Toward Beloved Community

Our goal is to create a beloved community and
this will require a qualitative change in our souls
as well as a quantitative change in our lives.

—MARTIN LUTHER KING JR., 1966

ANTIRACISM CONCEPT
**Beloved Community**

Our understanding of antiracism—and the thrust of this entire hand-book—is indebted to Martin Luther King Jr.'s references to "Beloved Community" as a goal for all of humanity. Though Dr. King did not originate this term, he embraced it as a key message. The vision of Beloved Community we hold is a vision of the radical inclusion of all human beings.[9] Beloved Community asks us to imagine that each person we encounter is a cherished member of our family. We want them to thrive as much as we want ourselves to thrive.

In this Beloved Community, just like in an ideal family, we are fiercely committed to the ongoing examination of the systems around us, to ensure they are meeting the needs of everyone, not just ourselves. In an ideal family, parents make sure their children are fed; they would not attend only to their own hunger. If we saw a family member doing so—letting their children or siblings or grandparents go hungry while they fed themselves—we would pay attention and try to address the situation. We would put our efforts toward helping feed the hungry child and work with the parents to remove any barriers so they could manifest the care that we trust is there. In Beloved Community we seek to create a new status quo: a status quo of genuine mattering, generosity, and interdependence. In Beloved Community our goal is an unflinching willingness to show up authentically and have difficult conversations as often as necessary to restore true well-being and harmony. As we try to fix broken systems and address inequities, we commit to persevere in dialogue, from a compassionate stance, until we arrive at strategies that truly work for all.

The idea of Beloved Community is grounded in our interdependence. As Martin Luther King Jr. wrote in *Letter from Birmingham Jail*: "I am cognizant of the interrelatedness of all communities and states.... Injustice anywhere is a threat to justice everywhere. We are caught in an inescapable network of mutuality, tied in a single garment of destiny. Whatever affects one directly affects all indirectly."[10] As we adopt the consciousness of Beloved Community, we move closer to an antiracist society. We recognize that even if we have benefited from white supremacy culture and other systems of social inequality that privilege some of us, we are never fully thriving if other folks are being left out. We recognize that even as we work to challenge these structures and free our communities from the constraints of white supremacy ideology, we can only be free when all communities are free.

Now that we have more of an understanding of Beloved Community, the question arises: Do we actually want it? The "Do I Actually Want Beloved Community?" questionnaire allows you to inquire into this for yourself. The answers are not scored as they are quite deep and tend to evolve in complexity over time. This questionnaire can be revisited many times and can help us see the development of our commitment to a different world.

QUESTIONNAIRE
## Do I Actually Want Beloved Community?

☐ Does the impact I've experienced or witnessed from systemic racism block me from even wanting to consider the humanity of those who have embodied white supremacy culture and taken harmful action, consciously or unconsciously?

☐ Is there anyone I see as outside my community, and as irredeemable?

☐ If so, do I like living this way?

☐ Is there anyone whose actions or behavior I find unquestionably evil?

☐ If so, does this take a toll on my body that I'm tired of?

☐ Do I believe that my liberation and the liberation of my community depends on everyone thriving? On everyone mattering?

☐ Do I value connecting to the shared needs motivating all behaviors, even those I find challenging?

☐ Do I want a more expansive vision of what is possible?

☐ Can I envision a world where things are very different, and am I willing to work for it, and even to live it, while the world continues to be in chaos and turmoil?

☐ Am I willing to take action aligned with my vision, even if I might not be the one to harvest the fruits of that action?


Assuming the answer to the question of wanting Beloved Community was at least a tentative or qualified "yes," what is next?

The work to dismantle racism and create truly equitable societies occurs in several spheres. We must change the policies and structures that prop up racism. In *Stamped from the Beginning*, Ibram X. Kendi demonstrates compellingly how racist ideas emerged to justify the policies enacted out of the self-interest of European traders, thereby formulating the societal institutions and structures that perpetuated social inequality. In order to end racism, he argues, we need to eradicate racist policies.[11] Antiracist efforts aimed at changing policy are essential. The work does not stop there, however. All too often, those involved in policy work have an us versus them stance fueled by a scarcity mind-set. Instead of working together to create better conditions for all, some groups fight bitterly to secure and maintain their bit of the pie at the expense of other groups. The disclosure in 2022 of racist, anti-Black remarks by Latine members of the Los Angeles City Council was a dramatic example of this. The news service *Vox* reported that the racial remarks were fueled by a "desire to siphon power away from Black Angelenos and other minority communities to ensure…a 'little Latino caucus of, you know, our own.'"[12]

Consciously choosing how we relate to each other, as we do the necessary advocacy and policy work to create systemic change, goes hand in hand with antiracist work. Without a clear vision of both how we can be in community together across differences and what we are working toward, we are likely to still operate on prevailing social norms based on white supremacy culture. Beloved Community offers an alternate vision that counters the values of white supremacy culture that we can use to guide our conscious behaviors and choices. Something that helps us connect with our own desire for Beloved Community is an understanding of human needs—the values and physical imperatives that motivate all human behavior, regardless of our culture or location. For example, unless we are in touch with our needs for inclusion and care, we won't even know that we would like Beloved Community to exist. It is only by allowing ourselves to feel our own longings for everyone to belong and remembering our interdependence that we will be able to create ongoing strategies and policies that are inclusive and potentially win-win.

JOURNALING PROMPT
## Your Own Beloved Community

Look at the "Needs and Values" chart in the Appendix (Figure 6). Describe the world you would like to live in. For example, how would people deal with conflict or make decisions? What would belonging look like, and how would people know they belonged? Which needs feel most important to you when you think of Beloved Community?

_____

_____

_____

_____

_____

_____

Holding your particular dream of Beloved Community in mind, let's look at the importance of belonging for human neurobiology.

NEUROSCIENCE CONCEPT
## Inclusion versus Exclusion

The need for belonging is so profound that it shapes our entire human experience. It affects how well we read one another's emotions, how quickly our hearts beat, what our body temperatures are, how often we get sick (and how quickly we get well), and whether we can relax, digest, play, work, and create. When we have a strong sense of belonging, mattering, safety, and welcome, we have an easier time understanding others, and our heart rates calm and become responsive to laughter and to sadness. Our body temperatures cool because we get to share our body heat, we get fewer colds and recover more quickly, we fully digest our food, and we can move seamlessly between play, work, and creativity.[13]

Every person and organization can have an effect. Each small gathering of people is a fractal of the larger whole; the larger whole is comprised of the many millions of smaller gatherings. Our families, communities, schools, hospitals, places of worship, workplaces, and government agencies can reassess what equitable inclusion and participation look like. Instead of working to ensure that people from the Global Majority gain access to spaces that were previously reserved for white people (and the colonialist, white supremacist, patriarchal, and ableist rules that govern those spaces), we can open ourselves to being in the work of re-creating together what our spaces should look and act like.

If we either only attend to the needs of white people or if we (prematurely) hope we already live in a postracial world, the social systems we engage in (health care, legal, economic, electoral, etc.) may default into the unconscious (or sometimes quite intentional) deprioritization of the Global Majority. White people and Global Majority people can act from this default programming. Even those not intending to do so may—unless they consciously pay attention to who they choose, serve, hire, and promote (and who they are assuming is the audience for their services)—unconsciously favor people who look and sound like themselves (the in-group) and harm people who don't (the out-group).

ANTIRACISM CONCEPT
## Recognizing Violence

Since noticing violence is the first step in interrupting and ending violence, let's explore what violence is. Many people assume violence is limited to physical actions (e.g., hitting someone) or verbal expressions (e.g., yelling, cursing). These actions are a small subset of the ways violence presents. Think of violence as the negative impact we experience from a person or group's attempt to address their unmet needs. Violence can occur intrapersonally (on ourselves), interpersonally (between individuals), and structurally (through systems and practices). Depending on our history, we may find it easier to recognize violence when it occurs in one sphere but not in another. For instance, an adult who had very critical parents and internalized their own harsh inner critic may be sensitive to and guard against interpersonal violence. But they might not assess their own derogatory self-talk as violence, instead arguing that such talk motivates them to do better.

Similarly, we often can recognize structural violence—harm to individuals and groups arising from the institutions and practices governing a community—when it impacts us but not pick up on examples of structural violence that impact others. For instance, the administration and staff at a school, some immigrants from non-English-speaking countries, recognized language comprehension was a barrier to equity. They carefully translated materials and had interpreters present at all events to reduce barriers to comprehension that excluded some families. They were less able to recognize and modify other practices that also excluded some families. The school's tradition of dressing up for "Community Spirit Day" meant families with less economic resources often did not have the capacity to purchase costumes, resulting in their children's exclusion from the very activities designed to increase inclusion and belonging.

Violence can impact us physically, emotionally, mentally, or spiritually. Our colleague, Edmundo Norte, combines these four aspects of human experience often described in Indigenous traditions and represented through the Medicine Wheel with the three areas of influence (intrapersonal, interpersonal, and institutional).[14] Roxy has combined forms of violence with Norte's integrated model. Most people readily recognize examples of physical violence occurring at each level (e.g., self-harm, negative self-talk, or substance abuse at the intrapersonal level; fist fights or sexual coercion at the interpersonal level; and voter suppression, war, or genocide at the structural level).

Other forms of violence are not always as easily identified. Mental violence at the intrapersonal level is often dismissed and indeed can be encouraged by capitalist entities. The mindless consumption of media exemplifies a form of intrapersonal mental violence in which many of us engage. If you've ever felt depressed over lost productivity after what you intended to be a quick online search for information somehow turned into an hour of scrolling Facebook, you might be experiencing the effects of intrapersonal mental violence. We might participate in structural violence when we enforce policies that result in harm to others. One example is school lunch shaming, when adult workers enforce rules that deny food or food of their choice to schoolchildren with unpaid lunch bills by throwing away the food rather than letting the child eat it.[15]

WORKSHEET
## Recognizing Violence in Our Lives

We regain choice and capacity to care for ourselves when we recognize how violence impacts us. In this worksheet you will explore impact both as the person impacted by violence and the person who enacted violence. Almost all of us, regardless of the identities we hold, have experienced being in both positions. As you complete the "Recognizing Violence in Our Lives" worksheet, notice where it is easier to recognize violence. Think about the words, behaviors, and policies you have encountered that have resulted in unmet needs for you. See if you can identify an example in each category.

*Examples of Violence I Have Experienced*

|  | Intrapersonal | Interpersonal | Institutional/Structural |
|---|---|---|---|
| Mental |  |  |  |
| Physical |  |  |  |
| Spiritual/Cultural |  |  |  |
| Emotional |  |  |  |

Now think of words or actions you have engaged in (including up-holding policies) that negatively impacted others. If you are unable to think of a time when you have enacted violence, consider asking people you trust to authentically share with you the impact they may have experienced. Use of this framework may become clearer as you work with the material in this handbook.

*Examples of Violence I Have Enacted*

|  | Intrapersonal | Interpersonal | Institutional/Structural |
|---|---|---|---|
| Mental |  |  |  |
| Physical |  |  |  |
| Spiritual/Cultural |  |  |  |
| Emotional |  |  |  |

ANTIRACISM CONCEPT
## Choosing Nonviolence

In his biography of Mahatma Gandhi, Eknath Easwaran wrote: "Satya and ahimsa, truth and nonviolence, became Gandhi's constant watchwords. In his experience, they were 'two sides of the same coin,' two ways of looking at the same experiential fact....Ahimsa does not contain a negative or passive connotation as does the English translation 'nonviolence.' The implication of ahimsa is that when all violence subsides in the human heart, the state which remains is love. It is not something we have to acquire; it is always present and needs only to be uncovered."[16] Nonviolence, as practiced by Gandhi and Dr. Martin Luther King Jr., who was inspired by Gandhi, involved an intention to do no harm. This is a grounded, thoughtful approach to nonviolence rather than an unconscious contract. This commitment is grounded in the awareness that harm can happen through positive action as well as through inaction. When we knowingly choose actions or fail to respond to actions that we are aware will result in harm, we are consciously choosing not to act in alignment with nonviolence. Why might we do this?

Nonviolent Communication invites us to hold that every action that a person takes is their best attempt, within the constraints of their capacity or awareness, to meet a need. Sometimes we are unable to identify any other way to attend to what we value than to take an action that might harm someone else. Sometimes the impact of white supremacy culture may lead us to devalue, justify, or dismiss the harm that is happening to others. When we choose nonviolence, we are making a commitment to seek other ways to get our needs met that do not harm others. We might choose to resist complying with institutional policies (like redlining) and structures of social inequality (being followed in a store by security because of your skin color) that cause harm. We can be supported in making this choice if we develop a practice of looking at the places where we are causing harm, consciously or unconsciously, and exploring what needs our actions are meeting. We can then attempt to find other strategies that can better meet our needs.

Consciously or unconsciously, as we move through life, we will take actions that result in harm for other people. Later in this handbook, we will discuss what to do when we recognize that someone has been impacted by our actions, whether those actions were intentional or unintentional. Often, harm occurs without our conscious intention or awareness. Even with the best of intentions, with our firmest commitment to Beloved Community, we can learn that we have impacted someone in a harmful manner. People who attend Roxy's course on microaggressions often respond with hopelessness. They exclaim: "I won't ever be able to do anything right" or "I'll never know what's going to offend someone or not." This sense of overwhelm can turn into passivity: "Unless I know and can avoid every possible way someone can receive impact, there's no point in trying."

This stance does not liberate us. It is certainly true that there is no way to know everything we must know in every moment to avoid ever stimulating harm. There are several steps we can take to cope with this truth. First, we must accept that there are things we do not yet know and commit to a practice of continuous learning. As I, Roxy, write this handbook and talk with members of my community, I repeatedly become aware of gaps in my understanding and ways I impact others that I did not previously see. Each time, as I stay open to my impact, I gain one more bit of information that will allow me to reduce my impact as I move through the world. As I reflect on my current behavior, I realize I am no longer doing the things I used to do that stimulated pain. Recognizing this helps me trust that with each new awareness, I can learn to do less harm to self and other.

Next, a corollary of the idea that we are continuously learning is that I can commit to a stance of curiosity and humility. Too often, when we are told we have impacted someone, especially when the impact was unanticipated, we defensively question the person. Did they understand what we were trying to do? Are they certain of the impact? Instead, we can remind ourselves: "Sometimes I have an impact I did not intend. I choose to listen and understand more about how this person was impacted and what I can do to support them." If we accept that harm does happen, despite our best intentions, and that it does not mean we are "bad," we have more spaciousness to be with the person impacted and with ourselves. Our curiosity and humility afford us the capacity to repair the harm that was done and therefore to do less harm overall.

WORKSHEET

## From Violence to Nonviolence

Choose an example of violence you have consciously or unconsciously committed. If you haven't already, you may wish to complete the "Recognizing Violence in Our Lives" worksheet to identify one.

What is the action or inaction?

_____

_____

_____

What needs were you attempting to meet by that (in)action?

_____

_____

_____

Did you experience harm as the result of your (in)action? If so, describe the harm. What needs were not met for you?

_____

_____

_____

Did another person experience harm as the result of your (in)action? If so, describe the harm. What needs were not met for that person? What needs were not met for you in relation to that person's experience of harm?

_____

_____

_____

Brainstorm at least one way you could meet your original need that would not result in harm to yourself or the other person.

_____

_____

_____

If you are unable to identify an alternative strategy, reflect on the ideals of nonviolence and Beloved Community. What needs would you meet by choosing not to take action to meet your original need? How would doing so support your intention to work toward Beloved Community?

_____

_____

_____

As you reflect on this practice, are there insights you want to remember to help guide future decisions? Write them here.

_____

_____

_____

 NEUROSCIENCE CONCEPT **Unconscious Contracts and Beloved Community**

As we will see throughout this handbook, the more conscious we are, the more powerful we are. When we experience difficulties alone, we often survive them by making promises to ourselves that we are quite unaware of. This happens because the part of our brain that stores difficult memories, the amygdala, has no sense of chronological time and really wants to protect us from ever making a "mistake" again. So it takes a behavioral response to a difficult event and links it to the frightening stimulus. We can call these habits "unconscious contracts." Here are some examples:

- When having to interact with a new boss, after having had a bad experience with a prior instructor, the old contract will come alive again: "I will never trust anyone in authority."
- When feeling overwhelmed and being told to ask for support, after having been shamed for being needy as a child: "I will only rely on myself."
- When imagining sharing vulnerably, after receiving life-long messages of unworthiness: "I will never let anyone know what I really think."

If we just stop there, accepting these statements as truth, they seem complete and unchangeable. But if we are able to dig a little deeper, we can discover that each statement is actually an unconscious contract that we've made, which links into a past or present difficult event that has simply been a part of our life experience. The way that we are able to do this excavation is with the very simple but powerful phrase "in order to." For example:

- "I will never trust anyone in authority *in order to* protect myself from the betrayal of my third-grade teacher."
- "I will only rely on myself *in order to* keep my heart from being broken as it was when I was eight."
- "I will never let anyone know what I really think *in order to* keep myself safe from my siblings' ridicule."

Bringing in the deeper work of "in order to" allows our bodies to communicate to us about what happened in the past—and how we found a way to survive it. Once we have a sense of *why* we've been doing what we do, we can check for truth by adding to the end of the sentence "no matter the cost to myself." As we say the full sentence, including that last phrase, we pay attention to feeling if our body says: "Yes, that's what I do." (Once we are able to fully name the contract and make sense of it within our personal history, we gain a new agency: to release ourselves from the contract, if we are ready.) As we will see, for members of the Global Majority, these kinds of contracts limit expression and a sense of wholeness, as well as the hope that Beloved Community is possible. For white people, these kinds of contracts underpin many of the harmful behaviors associated with white supremacy ideology and limit the capacity for Beloved Community.

 **QUESTIONNAIRE How Do I Unconsciously Limit Beloved Community?**

Many people have unconscious contracts that obstruct Beloved Community. Some of them may involve looking through a lens of right/wrong or good/bad, where people who act like us are "good" or "right," while people who appear to be different are judged as "bad." We may even lose sight of our shared humanity. Becoming aware of our contracts allows us to free ourselves from them and to welcome everyone into Beloved Community. You may wish to put a check mark next to any of these statements that ring true for you:

☐ "I will only consider people who see the world the way I do as belonging to my community."

☐ "When I meet people who treat me and others as less than human, I will consider them to be beyond redemption and unworthy of my time."

☐ "I will punish people who do not share my values by cutting them out of my circle of care; they will no longer exist for me."

☐ "I will not value or respect people who do not share my integrity."

☐ "I will not see or include people who look different from me."

☐ "I will not see or include people who have less than me."

☐ "I will not see or include people who have more than me."

☐ "I will believe that Beloved Community is a naive and dangerous concept."

☐ "I will believe that the part of myself that longs for Beloved Community is naïve and misguided."

As you find the statements that are truest for you, self-compassion is essential. People may find it unbearable to recognize that they believe some of these things, because they judge these beliefs as wrong. This "shame-trap" stops antiracism work in its tracks. If we can be immensely tender with our beleaguered brains, we will be more likely to discover the origin of our beliefs and release ourselves from our contracts. That liberation allows us to engage more effectively in antiracism work. Let's try adding "in order to" to contracts related to Beloved Community. Here are some examples. Yours may be different.

"I promise myself that I will punish people who do not see the world the way I do by cutting them out of my circle of care *in order to* have some power in a corrupt world that seems too big for me to change, no matter the cost to myself."

"I promise myself that I will believe that Beloved Community is a naïve and dangerous concept *in order to* keep myself safe from hope and heartbreak, no matter the cost to myself."

"I promise myself that I will not see or include people who look different from me *in order to* have familiarity and comfort and to be able to think that I understand the world and that it is predictable, no matter the cost to myself."

Now that you see the possible "in order to's," what happens to your self-compassion? What happens to your conviction that these contracts are permanent and unchangeable?

The final steps related to working with unconscious contracts are the release and the invitation. For the release we simply say to ourselves: "I release you from this contract." Then we add the invitation: "And instead, I invite myself to...." The invitation will make the original contract doable. For example: "I invite myself to claim my power without excluding others," or "to know that hope and heartbreak are just the human condition, and they will not destroy me," or "to know and accept that the world is not predictable, but that I can be predictable inside it," or "to recognize that excluding certain people does not make me safer."

### EXERCISE  Release the Contracts That Prevent the Intention to Live in Beloved Community

I, (YOUR NAME HERE), make a promise with myself that I will:
*(Insert one of the contracts that seemed true for you from the "How Do I Unconsciously Limit Beloved Community?" questionnaire.)*

_____

_____

_____

Then use the "General Worksheet to Release Unconscious Contracts" to release any of the unconscious contracts that feel true to you.

### IN CLOSING  Taking Beloved Community as Our North Star

These worksheets, exercises, and journaling prompts offer ways to make Beloved Community a shared North Star to guide us toward a

better world. Sometimes what we are reaching for is a little better—
and sometimes a lot better—than what is happening right here and
right now. For this journey we need nourishment, we need inspira-
tion, and we desperately need self-compassion to let our bodies continue to receive support while we access our fierce commitment to
creating an antiracist world.

In Chapter 2 we explore the various ways that white supremacy
culture affects our capacity to take accountability for our impacts,
seeks to squash the power of our righteous anger to fuel change in
service of Beloved Community, and keeps us tied up in harmful dualistic thinking. In addition, we are going to clear the way to bring our
anger—even our rage—into alignment with our longing for justice,
presence, integrity, and love. Such a shift can give us power.

# 2

# White Supremacy Ideology, Anger, and Love

 **ANTIRACISM CONCEPT**
**White Supremacy Culture**

White supremacy culture has at its roots the fallacious idea that white people are the epitome of all that is good, desired, and normal in the world. This belief in the supremacy of white people and white culture hinges upon the contrasting belief that Black people are the nadir of all that is bad, ugly, and wrong. These ideas largely evolved to justify the continued enslavement of Black people for the benefit of white nation-building, economy, and business. Encouraging widespread adoption of these beliefs, which characterized Black people as chattel rather than as human, made it possible for many people to accept and participate in the horrific cruelty of the institution of slavery without challenging it.[17] In addition, whiteness was characterized not only as an identity with accompanying privileges but as property imbued with legal protections and rights.[18]

White supremacy culture continues to permeate society today. It has shaped communities around the world and is encoded in the social and institutional systems that govern our lives, such as education, health care, housing, law, politics, and more. These ideas can manifest in both subtle ways (e.g., dashikis or saris being labeled "ethnic" clothing and used as costumes) and overt ways (e.g., braids or locs being deemed dirty and grounds for dismissal from employment). All of us, both Global Majority people and white people, learn these ideas and behaviors as we grow up. They are ubiquitous. Without a concerted effort to examine our thinking and actions and to explore the implications of our unconscious belief systems, we will inevitably act according to them.

**JOURNALING PROMPT**
## You and White Supremacy Culture

Think of the systems with which you engage daily. How do you get your food? How do you move around your community? Where do you go to school? How do you get care when you are sick? What are some ways white supremacy culture—a belief that white folks are better than other groups of people—show up in that system?

EXAMPLE: When Emily went to the Walgreens store in Silicon Valley, she was delighted to see how many available parking spots there were right next to the entrance. When she went to a Walgreens in a Black Oakland neighborhood, she was dismayed to see that the closest spot in front of the store was reserved for police cars. The store's policy reflects the white supremacy idea that Black people are criminals.

Your experience:

_____

_____

_____

_____

_____

_____

Think of your interpersonal interactions. What are some ways you might display white supremacy thinking in your words or actions?

EXAMPLE: <u>Anna enjoys going out to eat at restaurants with friends.</u> <u>When encouraging them to join her at an expensive restaurant, she simply</u> <u>said that they would be going to a French restaurant with a new chef from</u> <u>France because she knew everyone would understand it would be expensive.</u> <u>When inviting her friends to join her at an expensive Ethiopian restaurant,</u> <u>she explained that it was "elevated" Ethiopian food from an award-winning</u> <u>chef to justify the expense. Anna showcased a white supremacy culture be-</u> <u>lief that anything European is worthwhile while anything Black is cheap and</u> <u>poor quality unless it is an example of Black exceptionalism.</u>

Your experience:

_____

_____

_____

ANTIRACISM CONCEPT
## Understanding Anger Rules

Anger in the face of injustice and oppression makes sense. Anger lets us know that something we care deeply about is not being attended to. It is a signal that an important need is going unmet and that we need to take action to address that lack. Given this purpose of anger, it becomes clear why anger has been vilified in societies shaped by white supremacy culture and other forms of oppression. Those societies are structured so that entire groups of people systematically and profoundly do not have their needs met.

In many cases, those enacting the oppression are physically fewer in number than those being oppressed. If the oppressed groups tapped into their anger and allowed it to motivate them to unite and mobilize for change, they would be unstoppable. As a result, anger is demonized as not permissible in oppressive systems. Enslaved Black people who displayed anger were punished and even killed. In the Jim Crow South any sign of anger warranted a beating or worse. Women who show anger are judged much more harshly than men who show anger in a patriarchal society. And today, demonizing anger is still used to keep groups silent. For example, the descriptor "angry Black woman" is used to describe and shame Black women who protest the conditions in which they and their communities continue to live, as an effective strategy to silence Black women and sideline their concerns.

In the following table Dr. Myisha Cherry demonstrates how white supremacy beliefs shape the implicit rules about anger between white people and Global Majority people.[19]

| White supremacy beliefs | Corresponding anger rule for Global Majority people |
| --- | --- |
| Whiteness is superior to any Global Majority identity. | We cannot get angry about examples of white supremacy ideology. |
| Whiteness is entitled to special privileges. | We cannot get angry about the unequal distribution of resources to white folks. |
| Only people who have value can be respected. Anger is a justified response of those who are disrespected. | Since only white folks have value, anything done to Global Majority folks cannot result in justified anger since they cannot be disrespected. |

As white supremacy culture has infiltrated all of society, anger rules have infiltrated all our interpersonal interactions. People interacting in a society with these rules learn to apply them in any situation where there is a power difference as a way of enforcing power. Parents constrain and punish their children's anger. Anger in the workplace is deemed unacceptable. Without an understanding of the life-serving function of anger and healthy models of how to express anger, many of us fear anger. We attempt to suppress it or use it in ways that harm, thereby reinforcing the judgments against anger. In order to challenge the structures of racism, we must reclaim anger and its purpose. If we think of anger as something that is connected to needs and serves life, anger can be righteous. We use our anger to say: "No more! This must change." We can use our anger to protest the conditions that bind us, to stay energized in the face of fierce resistance to our efforts to change. But to do so, we must unchain ourselves from rules that have constrained us and do not serve us.

 **WORKSHEET**
**Exploring Our Anger Rules**

*Understanding the Origins of Our Relationship to Anger*

What rules about anger have you internalized?

_____

_____

_____

Who was allowed to be angry in your childhood?

_____

_____

_____

If you were ever allowed to be angry, what could you be angry about?

_____

_____

_____

How were you allowed to express your anger? What happened if you expressed anger outside the allowed format?

_____

_____

_____


*Exploring Anger in Society (Systemic Anger)*

What anger rules do you see at the systemic level?

_____

_____

_____


Which groups get to be angry?

_____

_____

_____


What differences have you noticed in how people from different ethnic groups are judged when they express anger?

_____

_____

_____


What are the costs of expressing anger for different groups?

_____

_____

_____

NEUROSCIENCE CONCEPT
## Life-Serving Rage

The discovery that we have emotional and motivational circuits that we share with all mammals was made by Jaak Panksepp, one of the most important neuroemotions researchers of the past seventy years.[20] According to Panksepp, there are seven different systems, or circuits, that run through the brain-bodies of all mammals. He refers to these circuits with capitalized letters to distinguish them from the ordinary use of the words. The seven circuits, as described by Panksepp, are SEEKING, CARE, PANIC/GRIEF, FEAR, RAGE, PLAY, and SEXUALITY.

We all have a RAGE circuit. We are all supposed to be able to get angry. This means (and this may be surprising) that access to anger is essential to our healthy functioning. Panksepp discovered that the only way to turn down the RAGE circuit without turning the volume down on all of our other circuits, which would cause us to lose access to our life energy, is to link our anger with our CARE circuit. When we feel anger, it can be supportive to start asking ourselves this question: What do we love so much, and want to protect so much, that it leads to anger when we perceive it to be under threat? When we know the answer to this, our RAGE circuit can start working for us in a life-serving way.

*From Roxy:*

Anger has always been a confusing emotion for me. Whenever I felt anger, I did not know how to express it or what to do with the energy. I usually stuffed it, distracting myself with books or food. While distraction successfully worked for many months at a time to keep me silent and complacent, the underlying need fueling the anger usually did not get met. At some point, seemingly without choice, I would explode. I remember destroying my brother's beloved watch in one of those moments of rage when I was a child. I would then judge myself harshly since expressing anger in that way meant not being aligned with deeply held values around care, harmony, and peace. I continue to work on trusting that I can harness the energy in my anger and express it, in service of authentic community.

*From Sarah:*

In my childhood, feeling angry was always something I had to apologize for. If I ever became angry, I was sent to my room and had to stay there until I wrote a letter of apology for hurting my mother's feelings. Even as an adult, I've always felt that anger was the worst thing I could possibly feel. Anger led to both an absolute loss of connection and then an absolute loss of self-respect. When I discovered that everyone has an anger circuit and that our anger circuits are integral to our flow of life energy, I had a lot of work to do to inform my nervous system that there could be a purpose for anger other than humiliation and disconnection, that there could be a rage that was life-serving and connected me even more deeply to my love. As I worked with my RAGE and CARE circuits, I began to understand that we need our life-serving rage—rage linked with love—to change the world.

To get a little closer to the idea of life-serving rage, we often have to spend some time acknowledging our own histories with other people's anger, and how they scared us with it. It may also be that we have scared our own selves or our parents or siblings with our anger; we can acknowledge this as well. Working from the journaling prompts earlier that explored your sense of personal and systemic anger, the "What Makes Me Angry? What Do I Love?" questionnaire is an opportunity to link your anger with the true roots of what makes you angry—your love.

## What Makes Me Angry? What Do I Love?

Circle what makes you angry in the list. How does your body feel when you think about what makes you angry? Draw lines from what makes you angry to what you love. How does your body feel when you notice what you love, and what beautiful values are at the root of your anger? The issues shown are Sarah's and may not accord with yours. There are blank lines after the list for you to add your own issues and your own loves.

| What Makes Me Angry? | What Do I Love? |
| --- | --- |
| Gerrymandering | Everyone's voice mattering |
| Banning education about enslavement | Bravery in the face of painful truth |
| A refusal to look at systemic racism | Courage and humility |
| Name calling and racial slurs | Integrity in speech |
| Ignoring, denying, or refusing to learn about microaggressions | Curiosity about how not to harm |
| Blaming society's problems on groups of people | Self-responsibility, ability to see the systemic racism |
| The inequalities of privilege | Societal thoughtfulness in policies |
| White fragility | The ability to see the big picture |
| Fake news | Peer-reviewed research |
| Laws that ban women's choice about their bodies | Autonomy, freedom |
| Laws that endanger the environment | Love for all the ecosystems of the planet |
| Policies/laws supporting fossil fuel extraction and use | All of Earth's plants and animals |
| Food deserts | Access to health and well-being for all |
| Cruelty to animals | Care and love |
| Global health and vaccine inequality | Commitment to each person mattering |

_____

_____

_____

_____

_____

What is it like for you to notice the deep love that lies beneath your anger? How does it change your body sensations to connect the two circuits of emotion, CARE and RAGE?

_____

_____

_____

_____

_____

Knowing how love and anger are connected can help us understand and accept the many ways that rage—our own and others'—shows up in antiracism. Learning not to fear our own anger, because we see its connection to love, can help us be with everyone's anger in a different, calmer way.

Many people with privilege respond to anger about systems from those with less privilege by trying to turn down the volume on their expression. They say things like "If they weren't so angry, it would be easier to understand them," or "You catch more flies with honey than with vinegar." This way of responding is called "tone policing." Humans are most likely to tone police when they have both privilege and unconscious contracts related to anger. Let's look at common blocks to self-compassion around anger and release any contracts that are blocking life-serving, life-changing anger and love.

COMMON BLOCKS
to Self-Compassion, Anger, and Love

Here are some of the unconscious contracts that people have that get in the way of accessing anger linked to love. Do any of these phrases resonate with you?

I will . . .

☐ never be angry
☐ never let anyone know I'm angry
☐ believe that I am not capable of love
☐ believe that love does not exist
☐ always suspect myself of ulterior motives
☐ not trust myself
☐ not know I exist
☐ not fully manifest
☐ not commit to this life

in order to . . .

- keep people safe
- keep from being accused of doing harm
- make sure not to do any harm
- make sense of my family of origin
- be loyal to my dad's criticism of me
- keep my own heart from breaking again
- stay with my family
- be in integrity with my dislike of this life
- stay with my brother who died

no matter the cost to myself.

EXERCISE **Releasing Unconscious Contracts That Block Anger and Love**

I, (YOUR NAME HERE), promise myself that I will:
*(Choose one of the phrases you just read that resonated with you.)*

_____

in order to:
*(Insert the words about anger and love that resonate for you.)*

_____

_____

Then follow the "General Worksheet to Release Unconscious Contracts" to release any of the contracts that feel true to you.

After doing the work of this contract release, how do you feel about yourself or others expressing anger about racism? Is it easier to guess at what love your own and others' anger has at its roots? It may be odd to imagine, but love is always the fuel behind anger, even when you don't know what it is that is being loved.

_____

_____

As we claim our own life-serving anger or rage, we become better able to also claim our collective desire to address and end systemic racism.

## Systemic Racism versus Interpersonal Racism

Racist systems, racist beliefs, and individual behavior work together and reinforce each other. We are all impacted by systemic racism, whether or not we are the direct target. As I write this handbook in 2022, proponents of racist redistricting laws attempt to disenfranchise Black voters, reducing their power at the polls. Voter suppression impacts not just people in those communities who lose their vote, but all of us who lose the benefit of a fully functioning democracy.

Systemic racism begets interpersonal racism. When a Black person walks into a store and is followed around, the individual store employee is assuming the Black person is a greater shoplifting risk than a white person: an assumption borne out of the racist ideas and policies that support our racist criminal justice system. Even the racial microaggressions that are a painful part of daily life for so many Global Majority folks are a form of interpersonal racism fueled by the racist ideas that support systemic racism. For example, systemic inequities clearly drive racial inequalities in educational outcomes. These are often not named; instead, the existence of inequities is justified by the racist narrative that the Black community does not value education. When someone compliments me by saying how exceptional it is that I earned a PhD and am so brilliant, they also share an underlying belief: "Black people don't value education so Roxy must be exceptional." A seemingly innocent compliment is actually a highly charged remark that reveals the speaker's unconscious feelings about Blackness, which have been shaped by white supremacy culture.

## to Connection in White Supremacy Culture

White supremacy culture entails certain beliefs widely accepted in modern society. While not explicitly about race, they work to create and enforce our separation and reinforce harmful stereotypes. Let's examine one of these blocks: dualistic thinking.

### Dualistic Thinking

The idea that there is such a thing as absolute good or evil, right or wrong, is a hallmark of white supremacy thinking. A belief in these sharp divisions, with no room for nuanced appraisal, made it possible to believe that Black is bad and white is good. Even those who explicitly reject white supremacy culture can unconsciously embrace binary thinking, even as they work to end racism. When we easily agree with the statement "All racists are bad," we demonstrate this world view. This perspective can be tempting because it seems to offer easy solutions to complex problems. But in reality it only reinforces problems we already contend with. Ultimately, when we are caught in dualistic thinking, we are blocked from seeing the full humanity of people who don't share our beliefs and from finding a path toward connection and understanding.

JOURNALING PROMPT
## Examining Dualistic Thinking

Think about a topic that you feel passionately about. Do you have strong beliefs about politics, gender identity, the existence of God, capital punishment, criminal justice reform, abortion, or any other topic? Select one of those topics and describe a person who you think would hold the exact opposite opinion to yours. Write about that person and why you think they hold those beliefs. When you finish writing, examine what you wrote. Look for signs of subtle judgmental language—for example, they are uneducated, they are intolerant, they are elitist. How hopeful do you feel about the outcome of a conversation with that person?

_____

_____

_____

_____

_____

_____

The rigidity and inherent violence of dualistic thinking often arises from trauma that people have lived through without accompaniment or resolution. Rigidity is the outer sign that we have unconscious contracts that try to compensate for never having had protection.

### IN CLOSING Countering Connection Blocks + Linking Anger with Love

Gaining understanding of the blocks to connection embedded in white supremacy culture makes it possible to counter them. When we recognize that we are all always impacting one another, we can begin working toward reconnection and repair. In this chapter we explored contracts about anger and how to link anger with love in order to find the fuel for fierce and compassionate antiracism. When we try to avoid our anger, our life energy dwindles and shrinks, and we can feel exhausted and overwhelmed. When we embrace our anger, we can use it to guide us to our heart's passionate longing and energize us to move toward what we deeply value.

In Chapter 3, in order to shift patterns of rigidity stemming from not having had protection, we look at trauma and its aftereffects. We also explore ways to hold ourselves with compassion.

# 3

# Time, Trauma, and Self-Compassion

NEUROSCIENCE CONCEPT
## Trauma Has No Sense of Time

People can use the words "trauma," "traumatic," and "traumatizing" to mean a lot of different things. In this handbook we use the word "trauma" to refer to the experiences that we've lived through that still activate pain, emotion, or sensation for us. This can include emotions like pain, anger, fear, loneliness, shame, or confusion. Such emotions are always connected to traumas. Sometimes we know which memories or traumas these emotions are connected with, but sometimes we just have the emotions without any conscious memories. Over the course of a life we will experience many difficult events (the loss of loved ones, physical injuries, betrayals, etc.). Events can become traumatizing if things happen too fast for our brains/bodies to integrate and if we feel alone with the experience. When the experience lives on in our bodies as a traumatic event, our bodies are not able to put it in the past; we are not able to fully know that the event is no longer happening. These aftereffects of trauma cloud our light and muffle our voices.

The more we know about trauma and how it can be healed, the more we can move toward our clarity, strength, and purpose. Our bodies can reveal how we are doing with the memory and what time frame the body is living in. When a memory causes our hearts to beat faster or causes a flush of shame to flood through us, this is a sign that the memory is still alive. Relational neuroscience teaches that such memories remain "alive" because we did not have the understanding and warmth that we needed to fully sort, store, and timestamp what happened to us. Even if there were a lot of people around, our brains will experience ourselves as having been completely alone if no one understood us. When we've been accompanied through even the most difficult events by another person, or internally by our own selves, with warmth and understanding, the memories don't hook us anymore and aren't traumatizing. As Certified Nonviolent Communication Trainer Olga Nguyen says: "Healing turns traumatic memories into life experience."

When distressing memories intrude into our lives involuntarily—perhaps as flashbacks, nightmares, or mental images, where it feels like they are happening in the present—they are called "intrusive memories." They are often a part of Posttraumatic Stress Disorder (PTSD). PTSD is the label for a mental health condition caused by experiencing or witnessing a traumatizing event. Other signs of PTSD could be difficulty sleeping, avoiding similar situations, changes in affect (emotional range or expression), and more. We might think intrusive memories are bad (or we may be very tired of those memories cycling and recycling), but the good thing about memories staying alive within us is that they remain available to be healed with accompaniment, warmth, and understanding, even decades after the events happened.

## NEW SKILL
## Time Travel

Time Travel processes are memory-resolution dialogues that allow us to both remain anchored in our present-day selves and let us access the past self that had the experience of trauma. Time Traveling to our past selves, the parts of us that lived through these intrusive memories, is surprisingly effective for healing. The only things we need to bring with us, to make our visit into the past a resolution of difficult memories, are our warm curiosity and our capacity for dialogue.

For people who belong to groups that have more power in their societies, two kinds of memories can spark shame and block self-compassion. The first kind is easier to find self-compassion for—a moment when we discovered that racism, systemic racism, or white supremacy beliefs existed in the people around us. This is trauma and an understanding of harm at the personal level. The second kind of memory presents more challenge. This kind—where we ourselves have been complicit in systemic harm, or when we suddenly discover the pervasiveness of the systemic harm—contains seeds of shame or shock that grow into the mighty invasive plants that block our self-compassion. Tending to both types of memories is vitally important for our healing and for empowering our antiracism work.

Let's see what happens if you Time Travel with warmth and a search for understanding to one of the moments when you learned that racism existed. Here are examples from both Roxy and Sarah, before you begin:

### Roxy's Time Travel #1
*Personal Work: Receiving Racism*

I was twelve or thirteen years old. I was in the bleachers in the school gym when a white boy said I had a nose like *Sesame Street*'s Snuffleupagus. Is it okay with the thirteen-year-old that I Time Travel to her? Yes.

She is in a freeze. I put everybody who's on the bleachers and in the gym into golden bubbles and float them up to the gym ceiling. All of a sudden there are these helium-filled balloons, golden balloons with people in them, and it's just us on the bleachers. I say to the thirteen-year-old: "Of course you froze."

The thirteen-year-old is feeling helplessness and shame. She is worried that they are right—that there is something wrong about my nose. And there is fear and confusion. In my family my brother has a bigger nose, so I never thought of myself as having a big nose. And I think the person who said this might have been someone I liked, so there is sadness. And what I needed most in that moment was congruence. It's something like—I was seeing myself as wonderful and then all of a sudden, I got this shock that I wasn't seen that way. How do I make sense of the world?

And here I am sitting with her in a Time Travel, and she has an intellectual curiosity about what I'm doing there. I tell her: "I'm here with you. And you don't have to feel numb with it. It did happen. And you don't have to pretend it's okay. I grew up to support people to understand and have compassion for their complex reactions to exactly this kind of thing."

I ask the thirteen-year-old if she wants to come home with me. And she does want to come home with me, to a world where kids are supported and understood for their complex reactions to things that happen.

Sarah's Time Travel #1
*Personal Work: Racism in Others*

I remember when I was about eleven years old, standing in my dad's workshop, smelling sawdust, and helping him hold a piece of wood that he was cutting with the table saw to build the stairs in our house. My father said: "When you grow up, I hope that you don't marry a Black man. It's easier to be married to someone you have a lot in common with." Remembering this moment, I feel bewilderment, shame, and anger.

In order to do this Time Travel, I need to not only be able to feel the aliveness of the emotions, but also to know that I'm now an adult who loves and understands my eleven-year-old self in this difficult moment. When I differentiate my grown-up self from my child self, I can turn toward the child with warmth and care. So I ask my eleven-year-old self: "Is it okay with you if I Time Travel to you?" She says: "Yes." As I come to her, I feel her lean into me for comfort, and I notice her shock. She has tears in her eyes.

We put my dad inside a golden floating bubble so that we don't have to worry about him, fight with him, or even think about him anymore.

"Eleven -year-old Sarah, do you feel shocked? Do you long for your dad's values to run all the way through him [another way of saying 'integrity']?"

She says: "Yes." She/I take a deep breath.

"Eleven-year-old Sarah, do you feel bewildered? Have you always seen your dad act with respect and inclusion for everyone?"

She says: "Yes, I'm confused about where his values have gone. It's like I've lost my dad."

And I ask: "Eleven-year-old Sarah, do you feel alarmed aloneness? Are you worried that you will grow up and fall in love with someone your dad doesn't want you to be with? And that the unconditional belonging that you've always felt with him will be lost?"

"Yes," she says. "And that I'll lose my dad, who I have loved most in the world. But at the same time, I feel contempt and anger, like I'll marry whomever I want to, and that his ideas don't make sense!"

"Oh," I say to her, "did something break inside you in this moment? When your father couldn't live up to the values he had always taught you, was this a moment of disillusionment and determination? Does it feel like you are a small piece of ice breaking off of a larger iceberg and floating away? Do you want to live in a different world than the one your father lives in? And at the same time, do you wish you never had to leave him?"

"Yes," she says. Her body relaxes. We hold hands and look at our father in the golden bubble. There is some pain in being separate from him.

"We get to live differently," I tell eleven-year-old Sarah. "We get to love differently. Would you like to come home with me?" And even though she is a big girl, she puts her arms up around my neck and her legs around my waist, and we step back through time and space to present time. I let her down and she melts into my heart.

Roxy's Time Travel #2
*Personal Work: Awareness of Systemic Racism*

One moment I viscerally understood systemic racism was when I was nineteen, in college. I was so proud of my English paper and was shocked to receive an F grade. I went to my professor's office to ask him why, and he accused me of plagiarism, saying: "Black people don't write like that." It's okay with the nineteen-year-old if I Time Travel to her. We put the professor into a golden floating bubble, and now he's bobbing against the ceiling of his office.

My nineteen-year-old self is feeling anger and tears. And frustration, and a whole swirl of shock and helplessness. There's a helplessness with the power imbalance. The professor has power over me, and there really isn't anything I can do.

I say to her: "Absolutely. Of course you're having these responses, this helplessness/hopelessness. Even when you do what's expected of you, you still fail."

"Yes," she says. "I fail if I'm too good, and I fail if I'm not. I'm supposed to do the best that I can and study hard and do all the right things. But if I do, I can be too good and then I'm accused of cheating. If I don't work hard enough, then I'm a lazy Black person. If I work too hard, then I'm a dishonest Black person. There's no way to be seen. It's an absolute dead end. There's no point in trying—people will come to their own conclusions, and what they decide won't have anything to do with me."

I didn't have the systemic lens at nineteen, so I ask my nineteen-year-old self: "Is it like there's no point in trying anymore? That no matter how much effort you put out, it won't be good enough? Did you walk into that meeting thinking there was a mistake and it would get straightened out? Were you still wanting celebration and companionship for the beauty of that paper? And now are you feeling crushed and hopeless because you want to be seen for who you are and cele-brated for what you can bring?"

She says: "Yes."

My younger self was still not wanting this to be what it was. She was still wanting to think she had some power to impact racism per-sonally, to escape from it. She had a naïve belief that she could do something to make things come out differently—that there would be some way that she could have enough power to change things. She was unable to recognize that this really wasn't about her.

I ask her: "Are you feeling trapped by the constraints? Is it like you see a box closing around you, getting smaller and smaller, squeezing you in, a box that says: 'This is how you can be Black in the world'?" I ask her: "Are you experiencing horrified hopelessness? Do you simply need freedom? Freedom and agency?"

"Yes," she says. "The box has taken away agency. It has taken away possibility."

My nineteen-year-old self is starting to realize the professor's be-liefs are truly not about any failure of hers; it's one impact of white su-premacy culture. She feels shame that she had that kind of judgment of others and that she had internalized it. That she was part of per-petuating white supremacy culture. At the same time, there is relief in a sad way. Before, she would always beat herself up about why she wasn't working hard enough or trying hard enough. Now she is say-ing: "Oh, it's not about me trying. I just don't have to try anymore."

As she says this, I remember some research that showed that Black children who understood about racism had an easier time making sense of the world. They didn't have to say: "I'm to blame. I'm the bad person." This was the moment that the shift in understanding was happening. She no longer had to beat herself up or think she was lazy or not trying hard enough. There was nothing else she could do to make things better.

I ask my nineteen-year-old self: "Are you needing awareness? How about support and protection so that there would be room for you to make mistakes like other kids? Time to still grow and learn? To have compassion and acceptance for who you are? Would you like the artificial blocks removed so that when you tried, you would get to see what you could do and how you could be?"

She says: "That's an interesting idea."

I tell her: "I came back to you because I'm writing these books. And I've gotten a lot of support in writing them. Even when I froze and didn't write as fast as I could, or I didn't think I was good enough, I had support. I came back so I could tell you the support will be there. The box doesn't stay closed. There are people who lift the lid and dismantle it."

I ask my nineteen-year-old self if she wants to come home with me and help me write. She says she just wants to come home with me, and although curious, watch from afar.

### Sarah's Time Travel #2
*Personal Work: Complicity in Systemic Racism*

I was fifty-four years old, participating in an exercise at an antiracism workshop being held in a huge hotel conference room. I brought all my conviction that I came from a low-income, subsistence-living, used-clothes disadvantaged family. I was sure that I wouldn't be separated from my Global Majority friend. In fact, I was sure that we had the same number of disadvantages (or even that I had more disadvantages!), given that my friend was smarter and better employed and had more financial stability than I had.

For the first exercise we were asked to stand in a line in the middle of the room. The facilitator read sentences from a list, each one describing a certain kind of societal advantage that various privileges afforded us. *Was it considered obvious that you were going to go to college? Were you able to get a bank loan with only one application? Do your parents own their own home? Did you grow up with books in the house?* We were to step forward if we identified with having that advantage and step backward if we did not. With each sentence that the facilitator spoke, I found myself moving further and further ahead of the group. When I looked back, I saw that my friend, who had been right beside me moments ago, was all the way in the back. I felt shocked and embarrassed. The shame of my advantages, and my lack of awareness of them, felt nearly overpowering. This is a moment that needs a Time Travel.

Does my fifty-four-year-old self consent to me time traveling? Yes. And we'll put all the other thirty-five people, including my friend, into golden floating bubbles.

I choose my feelings and needs. I ask myself: "Sarah, do you feel shock, shame, and bitter sorrow/horror that you've lived for so many years without understanding your advantages?" The answer is yes. The names of these emotions shiver through my body, starting to thaw the freeze from the traffic jams of these feelings, and I notice the immense tenderness that I have for my friend, off on the other side of the room.

I ask myself: "Do you need to stop time so that you can integrate this horror without doing any further harm? Do you need immense self-compassion for the layers and layers of sudden shame? Do you need accompaniment? Someone else who understands the bitter sorrow and horror, the sense of scales falling from your eyes? Someone else who has actually traveled this path, has compassion for you, and understands and mourns it with you?"

"Yes, yes, and yes. And I need a way to move forward with integrity, since it feels like all pretense of integrity has been stripped from me." There's something about realizing that I have been unknowingly living in an extended state of unconscious hypocrisy, by being in denial about both white supremacy culture and my participation in it, that is part of the experience of realizing the truth. I am now unprotected by my assumptions of economic hardship—suddenly I am a participant in and a benefactor of systemic racism. Fuck.

It's good for fifty-four-year-old Sarah to have me standing with her and understanding her. The thaw is spreading through my sensations in the memory. As she thaws, I ask her if she'd like to come home with me to six years in the future, where she can see what work I've done to integrate this moment of realization. Yes, fifty-four-year-old Sarah does want to come home with me—maybe I've made some headway with all this. We step through time and space, and she feels curious and wants to help.

When I think of the memory now, it doesn't stop me from breathing, and it feels like the experience—and working with it—has been part of what has brought me to where I am today, caring deeply about Beloved Community and working for antiracism.

Now that you have seen Roxy and Sarah both walk through this process, we invite you to try it with your present and past self, with the next journaling prompt and worksheet.

 JOURNALING PROMPT **Finding Difficult Memories Connected to Racism**

Spend a few moments reaching back into memory. When and how did you learn that racism exists? (This can be either as a Receiver of racism, systemic racism, and/or white supremacy ideology—you received harm from or were the target of the experience; or as an Actor/ participant—you realized that you had harmed or targeted someone else.) Try to recall specific moments when this shock of understanding that racism exists happened. Where were you, how old were you, who were you with? Examples of such memories might be when you became aware that racism was being directed at you, or when you realized you were directing it toward others. These incidents might be things that people said, times when people called you or others names, or when someone explained to you that something couldn't happen because of race. These memories might be moments when you realized others were making judgments or decisions about you based on race, or when you realized you were making judgments or decisions about others based on race. These incidents may also look entirely different than what is described here.

Let the three memories that are the most alive for you float to the surface and write them down in your journal. If you can find the willingness, remembering the most emotionally challenging moment of each memory can help you integrate and heal it. A part of this exercise is bringing up that particular moment in as much sensory detail as possible. If you choose only one moment, it helps to keep the memory from being intrusive or overwhelming. Spend as much time on each incident as feels right.

1. _____

_____

2. _____

_____

3. _____

_____

### WORKSHEET
## Time Travel

Choose one the memories from the previous journaling to work with here. How old are you in the memory?

Ask your younger self if it's okay to Time Travel to them:

☐ Yes        ☐ No

*(If "no," try one of the other memories that you wrote down. Does the self in one of those memories consent to you coming to visit with them?)*

*(If "yes," imagine stepping through time and space to be with your younger self. Is anyone else there in the memory? If there are other*

*people there, put them in floating, sound-proof bubbles so that you can focus on your younger self.)*

Look at the "Feelings" and the "Needs and Values" charts in the Appendix (Figures 5 and 6) and choose three feelings and three needs and values that look like they will most resonate for your younger self. In the memory, turn toward your younger self and ask them—

Younger self:

Do you feel _____

_____? *(write the feelings in here)*

And do you need or do you love _____

_____? *(write the needs in here)*

Now give your younger self the opportunity to answer. Does your younger self say "yes"? Or "no"? Does your younger self add any feelings or needs that you have not thought of? If your younger self is not completely relaxed, there may be more layers of feelings and needs that would like to be named. If so, you can pull up the "Feelings" and the "Needs and Values" charts in the Appendix (Figures 5 and 6) and try making a few more guesses.

_____

_____

_____

_____

_____

Would your younger self like to come home with you, and leave this time and place? If "yes," bring your younger self with you, and let this memory just become part of your life experience. If "no," ask your younger self where they would most like to be and bring them there (or leave them there) in your imagination.

How vivid is the memory now? Has anything changed in your body? What is it like to remember this incident? How does it feel, in your body, when you imagine sharing this memory with a close friend?

_____

_____

_____

_____

_____

_____

This process lets you explore one of the ways that accompaniment changes trauma into life experience. Another way to accompany our traumatized selves is to do the unconscious contract work that we learned about in the introduction and further explored in chapter 1.

 NEW SKILL **Self-Compassion**
(An Introduction to Self-Empathy)

Once we recognize that we all move through the world in ways that can have an adverse impact, we can learn how to work with that impact. In addition to releasing any vows that prevent us from acknowledging harm, we need to find ways to let go of the harsh good/bad judgments that white supremacy culture might induce us to make. Dualistic thinking can be a powerful block to self-connection. When we cannot hold ourselves with compassion, it becomes too painful to fully face any harm resulting from our actions and to stay in Authentic Dialogue with those impacted.

The self-compassion practice (known as self-empathy in Nonviolent Communication) invites us to use our awareness of our needs to understand actions, rather than apply an absolute metric of good or bad. When we see that our actions meet needs for us and for others, we might call that action "good"—in Nonviolent Communication we notice that needs are met and we feel satisfied with the outcome. Actions that result in many unmet needs for ourselves or others might be called "bad"—in Nonviolent Communication we notice that needs are unmet and we might feel dissatisfied with the outcome. Notice how different this can be from the right/wrong judgments that come out of dualistic thinking. In dualistic thinking, we easily judge our actions and thus ourselves as good or bad. In needs-based thinking, we judge how well needs are met or not met. We are not judging people, but the effectiveness of our strategies to serve life.

Self-empathy allows us to look at what motivated our actions—at what our intention was. The exploration into our intention is not meant to release us from any responsibility to attend to the harm. Instead, by connecting to the needs we were trying to meet, we can hold self-compassion and even appreciation for our beautiful intentions and can explore other strategies that we can try that would not be so costly. Understanding ourselves and our motivations provides a path to more intentional choices in the future. Self-empathy can also help us connect to our reasons for wanting to attend to the harm. Many of us are motivated to attend to harm from the right/wrong energy of white supremacy culture. Bad people cause harm; good people clean it up.

Even as we attempt to make repairs, that effort comes from and perpetuates the very dualistic thinking that is part of the problem to begin with. Instead, we can ask ourselves: *When I see this person who has been impacted by my actions, how do I feel? What needs do I experience when I notice this impact?* We might realize that we're feeling troubled because we value care and kindness. We may feel restless as we connect to our values for contribution and effectiveness. We may feel hope when we realize how important inclusion and accountability are to us. When we connect to these needs, we might move toward repair with a feeling of relief that there are things we can do that align with our values.

In the "Self-Empathy for Impact and Intention" worksheet you have a chance to try out self-empathy for yourself with a difficult memory—a memory of a time in which your action did not meet needs for yourself or others in a way that really satisfied you.

## WORKSHEET
## Self-Empathy for Impact and Intention

Identify a situation in which you were the Actor—a time when you took an action that resulted in an adverse impact for someone else. Describe the worst moment:

_____

_____

_____

*Self-Empathy for Impact:*

Begin by acknowledging your best guess at impact. After you fill in the blanks, read these sentences aloud:

"When I said/did *(describe action)* _____

_____,

I am guessing that it had this impact." *(describe impact)*

_____

_____

_____

Check in with yourself. Do you notice any feelings or sensations? You might look at the "Feelings" chart in the Appendix (Figure 5) for support. Ask:

"When I think of the impact I had, do I feel *(name the feeling)*?"

Pause and see if there is resonance—if your body responds or relaxes. If there is none, see if naming another feeling captures your experience. When you find the feeling, take a moment to notice it. You don't need to change it or shift it in any way; just notice how your body experiences the feeling.

Let your mind turn to needs. Do you notice any needs that are present? If you need help, scan the chart of "Needs and Values" in the Appendix (Figure 6) and see if any resonate with the feeling you are experiencing. Once you become aware of a need, ask yourself: "Am I feeling *(name the feeling you identified)* because I need *(name the need)*?"

Again, pause between each question and check for resonance. If you find resonance, you can answer yourself: "Yes, I am feeling *(name feeling)* because I need *(name need)*." Notice how your body responds when you acknowledge your feelings and needs.

You may find several feelings and needs that resonate.

*Self-Empathy for Intention:*

Now turn your attention to your original action. What feelings and needs did you have that led you to take the action? You might ask yourself:

"Was I hoping to meet needs for *(name needs)* when I *(name action you took)*?"

"Was I feeling *(name feeling)* about meeting my need for *(name original needs)*?"

Ask yourself: "Am I feeling *(name feeling)* as I think of *(name original need)*? How do I feel as I contemplate how well my action met my original need?"

*Next Steps:*

Think of all the needs you identified—your original needs and your needs in relation to the impact. Take a pause to let the needs percolate in you. Are any of these needs ones that you wish to attend to in this moment? (For example, speaking directly to the person to make a repair, or giving back resources that were taken away, or asking the person about what the impact was for them, etc.)

If a need to take action or connect with the person arises, ask yourself: "Am I willing to *(name action)* in order to attend to my need for *(name need)*?"

If your answer is "yes," then leave the handbook for a bit and take the action that seems important to you.

As you explore this worksheet, you might find it easier to sit with your feelings and needs in relation to your intention or to your impact. Try to give space for both. This humanizes both you and the person impacted and can help you access compassion for both.

IN CLOSING

## Claiming Power

In this chapter we've learned about how trauma lives in our bodies as an extreme emotional sensation, and how it can confuse our ability to differentiate between the past and the present, which blocks our clarity and self-awareness. Accompanying ourselves to transform trauma into life experience and using self-empathy instead of dualistic thinking allows us to move from guilt and shame into our actual power as humans and community members.

In Chapter 4 we learn about how privilege (power and immunity related to our position in society, including our whiteness) impacts brains and decreases empathy. This lens exponentially expands our understanding of how to practice antiracism with a full heart.

# 4

# Removing the Blinders of Privilege

ANTIRACISM CONCEPT
**Privilege and Centering**

US society was originally designed as a political structure to secure and maintain power and resources for white male landowners. In the country's founding, colonial white settlers set up systems that defined who could own property, who was a citizen, and who could vote. Throughout US history any time a practice threatened this white male power structure, new policies and laws have been enacted to maintain the white family's hold on power. Although the story of the United States is often told as one of freedom and revolution, that story is incomplete. One form of inequity quickly begat another: from the very beginning, this country has been built upon the necessary exclusion and exploitation of large groups of people for the sake of others' being "free."

As I, Roxy, write this handbook, it has been 417 years since the English first set foot on what is now Virginia.[21] And 417 years later, those of us who were not included in that initial charter's conception of who deserved to be free are still struggling for that freedom. By "freedom," I mean having full recognition of our sovereignty and control of our bodies, freedom from economic exploitation and cultural degradation, and unfettered access to political power. Being seen as fully human. The equal of any white man.

The history of the nation's founding informs our understanding of privilege. The *Oxford Pocket Dictionary* defines "privilege" as "a special right, advantage or immunity granted or available only to a particular person or a group of people."[22] During the founding and in subsequent years, many privileges were encoded into law that gave rights exclusively to white men. For instance, just before the 1700s, laws were passed in Maryland and Virginia that severely punished white women who had sexual relationships with men who were not white; white men did not have the same restrictions put in place.[23] White men had the horrendous privilege of having intercourse with and/or raping anyone they wished with little fear of punishment. However, if white women or Black men had interracial intercourse, they would not only be punished by the state but punished by their peers: many were murdered in the aftermath of such couplings.

Allocating privileges to white people continued through to the present day. Many living Black people vividly remember navigating the Jim Crow South. During that recent era, Black people had to ensure they did not attempt to sit in certain seats, go to certain stores, or attend certain schools. Access to these things were privileges granted to white people only. Some privileges are coded into law while others are part of the unwritten social code. The inequities inherent in the assignment of privileges are enforced with the penalty of jail or even death. In this way, privilege can either be explicit or insidious. As long as people continue to uphold the racist ideas that underpin white supremacy culture, they will continue to believe that some people deserve things that others do not.

Even now, despite the many laws enacted over the past half-century to protect Global Majority people from the inequitable treatment that white supremacy culture would mandate, white people still benefit from many exclusionary privileges. These privileges vary in size and scale. Roxy has experienced going into large chain stores in well-to-do neighborhoods and having to ask someone to unlock the case to purchase low-cost products designed for Black hair. White people shopping in the same stores can freely select their products without requiring supervision. Many studies show that white people seeking medical care are more likely to receive appropriate care and be treated with dignity; Black people continue to be underdiagnosed and undertreated, thus being more likely to die from preventable causes.

As they wrote this handbook, Roxy and Sarah talked about their experiences teaching their children to drive. Sarah experienced a privilege available to many white parents—trust that her child was unlikely to be harmed during a police stop. She taught her son that if he were driving at night and saw a police car behind him, he could turn onto the nearest side street and park so he would not be ticketed. Roxy, like many Black parents, did not have this privilege. She taught her children that in the same situation, they should drive to a well-lit place, always keep both hands visible on the steering wheel, and clearly state what they were doing before reaching for any identification.

The array of privileges afforded to white people in societies shaped by white supremacy culture range from simple ones that make life easy or more pleasant to significant ones that have life or death consequences. It is important to note that it is rarely the case that a white person asks for these privileges. The white woman entering the store does not say to the clerk when entering the store: "Hey, I'm white, you can trust me." Neither does the Black woman entering the store say to the clerk: "Hey, I'm Black. You should follow me around." People benefit from privilege with or without their consent and people are disadvantaged by racist practices with or without their consent. Although this may seem obvious, it is an important point to reiterate. The special advantages of privilege are available to those who are granted access to the privileged group, whether or not one asks for it and whether or not one accepts it.

It is certainly possible to refuse an unearned privilege. Roxy shares one example: "While waiting in line to be served at a store, it happens fairly commonly that a clerk approaches and begins speaking to a white customer who arrived after me. When that customer redirects the clerk to me, pointing out that I had been waiting longer, I feel relief." That is an example of someone who understood a privilege was made available to them and turned it down. Many people, however, don't even recognize when they have benefited from privilege. For instance, Roxy taught at a state university that had an Equal Opportunity Program that provided tutoring and coaching to low-income, first-generation, and Global Majority first-year students. Her Global Majority students noticed that their white peers who were not in the program attributed their ease of adjustment to college and higher grades to their own hard work. Many of these white peers had attended schools in middle-class or wealthy, predominantly white districts. These white students did not realize the special advantage they gained by attending well-funded high schools with Advanced Placement classes, going on college tours with their parents, or having parents or siblings who had already attended college and normalized the experience for them. Their privilege was invisible to them.

JOURNALING PROMPT
## Reflecting on Privilege

If you are a Global Majority person, recall a time when you have witnessed a white person receive a benefit or advantage that was not available to you. Describe what happened. As you reflect on the incident, recall how you felt at that moment. Feelings of anger and disgust are quite common as we watch people receive benefits denied to us. Or perhaps you felt sadness? Shame? We have a wide range of responses in these moments of exclusion from resources and experiences we desire.

Look at the "Feelings" chart in the Appendix (Figure 5) and select three words that match how you felt as you witnessed a white person receive the privilege you could not access. Next, explore the "Needs and Values" chart in the Appendix (Figure 6). For each of the feeling words, choose a need that stimulated the feeling. Write for a few moments, exploring your feelings and needs that you experienced. If you notice judgments coming up about the people in the situation, ask yourself, what value or need of yours is this judgment pointing to? See if you can identify what is important to you about that need. End the activity by journaling what needs were met for you by revisiting this incident.

_____

_____

_____

_____

_____

_____

If you are a white person, recall a time when you became aware that you were receiving an unearned advantage, or privilege, because of your whiteness. If you are not able to identify one, read the rest of this chapter then come back to this activity. You may find it easier to access a memory of such a time after exploring the neuroscience around privilege. Describe the event that you recall.

As you reflect on the situation, check in—how did you feel at the time that it happened? It's quite common for people to feel delight in the moment as they benefit from a privilege. It's also quite common to feel embarrassment, anger, or shame. Perhaps you felt something completely different. Look at the "Feelings" chart in the Appendix (Figure 5) and select three words that match how you felt as you received the privilege. Next, explore the "Needs and Values" chart

(Figure 6). For each of the feeling words, choose a need that stimulated the feeling. Journal for a few moments about the feelings and needs you experienced. End the activity by journaling about what feelings and needs you experienced as you revisited this incident.

_____

_____

_____

_____

_____

_____

After doing this exercise, both Global Majority people and white people might consider using the "Time Travel" activity to accompany their prior self with resonance.

NEUROSCIENCE CONCEPT
## The Impact of Privilege on Brains

How does privilege show up in our societies? If you are a tall, white, college-educated, employed, healthy, able-bodied, forty-year-old man with a full head of hair in Europe or North America, with a Christian family background who inherited money or property from your family, who likes women sexually and has enough money to own a house and a car, then you are at the pinnacle of having more advantages than other people. This gives your body more immunity from stress—from fear, from uncertainty, from ill-health, from losing your home, and from having to worry that your children will be harassed or carelessly shot by police.

While health increases with privilege, empathy does the opposite. Social psychologist and researcher Paul Piff has shown that the more social advantages a person has, the less likely they are to consider the needs of others. In his research Piff found that even access to temporary advantages make us believe that we are better than others. And he has found that socioeconomic safety makes people less ethical, more selfish, more insular, and less compassionate. The more power a person has, the more their brain tends to an unconscious bias against nonpower-holding groups.[24]

*From Sarah:*

Change any of the privilege descriptors listed previously, and you start to move away from the pinnacle. With each descriptor that is changed, by definition, you have less privilege (less advantage, less immunity) and experience more strata of oppression. In our scarcity-based society, most of our privileges come at the expense of others. Some have more precisely because others have less. For example, it has historically been easier for people legally defined as white to own homes and to pass on accumulated wealth. This did not happen in a vacuum: the ease with which white people were granted loans was possible precisely because it was made nearly impossible for those of the Global Majority to have access to loans. When my parents applied for a loan to buy their home, they were granted it easily, and with a good interest rate. My parents could have had all the same exact privileged qualifiers (education, income, family, etc.), but if they hadn't been white, they wouldn't have been approved for the loan they needed to purchase their home.

I benefit from this directly: because my parents were able to buy their home, they had a stable place to live and age, and I had the safety net of knowing that, were I ever to be in trouble, there was a stable place that I could go to be cared for. As homeowners (and not renters), they accumulated value in their home over their lifetimes and had wealth to pass down to their children and grandchildren. All of this directly impacts the life I have been able to live. Many people don't want to know this and even have unconscious contracts not to know. The tendency to *not want to know* results in white people as a group having a failure of imagination when it comes to the lives of the Global Majority. Since white people in most of the societies they live in have more privilege than others, many people's brains center whiteness, by which I mean that many people unconsciously make white people's needs the most important ones. Those of us who are white, and even some Global Majority people, don't even know how to notice that everything is revolving around the white experience. This means that white people rarely recognize that they are making themselves the center of all their own thoughts and actions.

This happens not because white people are bad, but because in the absence of concerted efforts to counter its effects, privilege hurts brains. When we have more privilege, research shows that we lose empathy and the capacity to imagine what is happening for those who have less privilege. Our brains are also very likely to reward us for the gifts of our birth or of chance by making us believe that we have received these gifts because we deserve them. This is particularly deadly because of the consequences of this belief on social decision-making. For example, people who believe they have earned their high status believe others have earned their low status. They are more likely to believe that the people with low status deserve punitive criminal justice. They are less likely to see the systemic factors at work or to advocate for social programs and policies that are more likely to effect change.[25]

One thing that happens to people who have privilege is that they can't feel it—all they can feel is the places where they lack privilege. They think, as I did, that their own personal experiences of lifetime hardship discount any of the systemic privileges they may have been afforded by being white. People say: "But I worked hard and sacrificed to become a surgeon. You don't know the number of sleepless days I had when I was starting out. You don't know that I was poor and lived in a trailer park." People are rarely able to immediately step into this conversation and say: "Oh, yes, I have privilege, it's true. I did work very hard and it was because of my whiteness that I was able to believe that if I worked hard enough, anything was possible. I can hold both."

Each layer of privilege increases the power people have. The more layers of privilege people have, the more social influence they have— the more power they have to form laws and shape what we call morality. The more power people have, the fairer they believe the world is, and (this brings us back to Piff's research) the more they tend to believe that they have earned their advantage. If we are white and have many different kinds of privilege, our response to this chapter may be protest. We might be clenching our fists or feeling tightness in our chests or wanting to say that this isn't true for us, that we see everyone in an equal and unbiased way. With privilege comes fragility, and when we talk about the existence of white supremacy ideology and structures, we also must talk about white fragility.

Robin DiAngelo developed the concept of white fragility.[26] A working definition is *the defensive reaction white people have when they receive information about their privilege and about systemic or personal racism.* This defensiveness serves to maintain the white person's innocence and lack of culpability for the effects of racism. White fragility includes denying systemic or personal racism; saying that the speaker is too angry, hostile, or absolute; expressing grief about the white person's good intention not being seen; focusing the conversation back on themselves or their own experience; and wanting to be seen for their contribution or allyship in order to minimize their responsibility for and benefit from a system that harms the Global Majority. This is not a complete list, just a basic outline and starting point for understanding the ways that defensiveness keeps us from connecting and learning.

WORKSHEET
## White Fragility

*For Global Majority folks:*

Think of the last time (there may be many moments!) when someone responded to you with white fragility. Freeze the white person and any Bystanders in your memory, and turn them upside down or make them disappear. Now, Time Travel, with great self-compassion, to your past self of that moment. Write down your body sensations in the moment of experiencing how white fragility impacts you. Keep your attention entirely on yourself. For each body sensation, find a feeling word from the "Feelings" chart and a needs word from the "Needs and Values" chart in the Appendix (Figures 5 and 6). When your body has relaxed somewhat, at the end of the process, ask your past self if they would like to come home with you to the present time, rather than having to stay in that memory.

Body sensation: _____

_____

Feeling: _____

_____

Need: _____

_____

Body sensation: _____

_____

Feeling: _____

_____

Need: _____

_____

Body sensation: _____

_____

Feeling: _____

_____

Need: _____

_____

Body sensation: _____

_____

Feeling: _____

_____

Need: _____

_____

*For White Folks:*

Think of a time when you may have inadvertently shut someone down in a moment of fragility and defensiveness. One important practice is to do a Time Travel to that moment and hold yourself with compassion for the choices that you made. From this place of compassion for the ways that brains with privilege, including yours, close themselves off to and have less empathy for others who have less, or who the brain perceives as "other," choose body sensations, feelings, and needs that you imagine *the people who received your words or actions* might have been experiencing (see the "Feelings" and the "Needs and Values" charts in the Appendix, Figures 5 and 6). If you find that you can't think of a response to this prompt, possibly because you don't remember ever having been fragile, please work through a few of your unconscious contracts in the next exercise and then return to see if a response becomes more available.

Body sensation: _____

_____

Feeling: _____

_____

Need: _____

_____

Body sensation: _____

_____

Feeling: _____

_____

Need: _____

_____

Body sensation: _____

_____

Feeling: _____

_____

Need: _____

_____

Body sensation: _____

_____

Feeling: _____

_____

Need: _____

_____


## The Unconscious Contracts of White Fragility

As mentioned earlier, we often make unconscious contracts to our-selves in order to survive difficult moments. These agreements hum under the surface and determine our behavior, even though we may not know of their existence. Excavating these agreements gives us insight into the deeper truths of how we are always trying to save our-selves or others, even when our attempts to save actually do harm.

Here is an unconscious contract that I, Sarah, recently found in my subconscious as I was working on this handbook: "I, Sarah, promise myself that I will be an exception to racism, that it won't apply to me, and that I will be racially innocent, in order to preserve my view of myself as good and in order not to have to belong to a group that does harm, no matter the cost to myself or to those I love." That was a good one to release. Once I found it, I asked myself if I wanted it. I didn't need it any longer, so I released it and I invited myself to be fully part of everything and to take responsibility for my part of the harm in my world. The "Which Contracts Try to Help Us Survive White Fragility?" questionnaire will help you explore possible uncon-scious contracts in regard to white fragility, both from the point of view of the Global Majority and from the point of view of those who are white.

 QUESTIONNAIRE **Which Contracts Try to Help Us Survive White Fragility?**

*For Folks in Positions with Less Racial Privilege:*

What are the contracts that have let me survive the white fragility of others? Here are some common contracts that help Global Majority people survive white fragility.

> *(Put a check mark next to the Contract Beginning that feels true to you and circle the "in order to" that feels right—or add your own. Then take your discoveries to the contract releasing exercise that follows.)*

Contract Beginnings: I promise myself that . . .

☐ I will not trust anyone who has privilege/is white

☐ I will live in a state of anticipatory contempt

☐ I will work harder than anyone else

☐ I will live as if racism didn't exist

☐ I will believe there is something wrong with me

☐ I will not waste my life energy

☐ I will devalue and set aside my needs

☐ I will protect and help white people

in order to *(in no particular order, and add your own)* . . .

- survive
- keep my heart from breaking
- not be disappointed
- not have to hope ever again
- not waste my life energy
- succeed
- make sense of a racist world

■  _____

■  _____

■  _____

no matter the cost to myself or those I love.

### For Folks in Positions of Racial Privilege:

What are my white fragility contracts? Here are some common white fragility statements (or thoughts) and the elements of the contracts that lie behind them.

> *(Put an X beside the statements that feel true to you, a checkmark next to the Contract Beginnings that seem accurate, and circle the "in order to" that feels right—or add your own. Then take your discoveries to the contract releasing exercise that follows.)*

If you don't identify as white but still want to look at these questions, you can review these contracts from any privilege that you have and substitute words: healthy, neurotypical, male, heterosexual, young, college-educated, financially well-off, able-bodied, and so on.

**White Fragility Statements: Wanting our intentions to be seen.**

_____ "How could you suggest that I could have said or done something racist or that I'm a white supremacist?"

_____ "I'm not a racist—I marched for Black Lives Matter and have a Black foster brother. I've always worked for racial justice, I contribute to voting rights organizations, and have always taught my children about the Civil Rights movement. I am an ally!"

_____ "I'm not racist. You are not seeing my good intentions."

_____ "I don't see color."

_____ "We're all just human! Race is a construction."

_____ "I don't support the system and I'm not part of the system."

Contract Beginnings: I promise myself that . . .

☐ I must be a good or kind person at all times
☐ I will always be conscious
☐ I will never make a mistake
☐ I will not forgive myself for social errors
☐ I will be perfectly socially graceful
☐ I will believe that I do not see color
☐ I will believe that because I do not intend harm, I do no harm
☐ I will believe that I'm exempt from being racist
☐ I will believe that my past contributions make me innocent today
☐ I will never let my intentions go unrecognized

in order to *(in no particular order, and add your own)* . . .

▪ serve God or the greater good
▪ be a good person
▪ survive
▪ not be kicked out
▪ belong
▪ be safe from humiliation and ridicule
▪ not belong to a group that does harm
▪ _____
▪ _____
▪ _____

no matter the cost to myself or those I love.

**White Fragility Statements: I have no power. I have received harm.**

_____ "I don't have any power or resources. I don't oppress anyone."

_____ "How could I be capable of doing harm when I have been so harmed?"

_____ "Life wasn't easy for me either! I grew up poor and worked for every single thing that I have: How could you say that I'm privileged?"

_____ "I guess I just don't matter to you."

_____ "When you say I have privilege, you aren't seeing me or my pain."

Contract Beginnings: I promise myself that . . .

☐ I will believe I am too insignificant to do harm

☐ I will not have any power

☐ I will not believe that I matter

☐ I will believe that I don't belong anyway, so how can I have any responsibility

☐ I will believe that I am always at the mercy of others

☐ I will never be the perpetrator

☐ I will believe that I am the injured one

in order to (in no particular order, and add your own) . . .

- make sense of how hard things have been
- not belong to a group that does harm
- not be a perpetrator
- not be like my father, who did me harm
- honor my journey and my family's journey
- defend the well-being of my children, family, and people like me
- keep myself safe
- _____
- _____
- _____

no matter the cost to myself or those I love.

**White Fragility Statements: I'm not the racist, you are!**

\_\_\_\_ "You're the one who's making this about race!"

\_\_\_\_ "Global Majority folks have the same opportunities I have. I earned my place. They just don't work hard enough."

\_\_\_\_ "Your obsession with your oppression isn't my responsibility."

Contract Beginnings: I promise myself that . . .

☐ I will believe that I am innocent

☐ I will believe that each person is responsible for their own well-being and experience/their own reality

☐ I will believe we are all on an equal playing field

☐ I will believe that I have what I have because I have earned it/worked so hard/came from nothing

in order to *(in no particular order, and add your own)* . . .

- make sense of my life
- do no harm
- take responsibility for my own life
- belong to my father or my family
- earn my belonging
- _____
- _____
- _____

no matter the cost to myself or those I love.

**White Fragility Statements: Don't shame me for white history!**

\_\_\_\_ "Critical Race Theory is brainwashing our children to feel bad about who they are!"

\_\_\_\_ "Enslavement and racism happened a long time ago. Things are better now!"

\_\_\_\_ "I will not feel ashamed of my history! I am proud of being American."

Contract Beginnings: I promise myself that . . .

- ☐ I will not talk about race
- ☐ I will believe that white people are under attack
- ☐ I will protect children from experiencing pain, shame, or blame about our country or their whiteness
- ☐ I will protect my reputation as a good person
- ☐ I will not let anyone criticize my country
- ☐ I will not see the level of inequality that exists in my country
- ☐ I will believe that white people are just people, and everyone else is a race
- ☐ I will believe that everything is fine as it is
- ☐ I will believe that seeing systemically invalidates personal power
- ☐ I will believe that this is not who we are

in order to *(in no particular order, and add your own)* . . .

- ▪ protect myself and others from shame and humiliation
- ▪ be a good person
- ▪ earn my father's love
- ▪ honor each individual and not leave them
- ▪ make sense of all the good people who have privilege
- ▪ _____
- ▪ _____
- ▪ _____

no matter the cost to myself or those I love.

**White Fragility Statements: Don't talk to me that way!**

_____ "The way you are speaking to me is disrespectful or violent."
_____ "Your tone is strident. You are too harsh."
_____ "You are too angry for me to speak with you."
_____ "You should have told me this in private."
_____ "It's the way you are saying it."
_____ "You're saying it wrong."

Contract Beginnings: I promise myself that . . .

☐ I will not be disrespected
☐ I will not allow anyone to speak to me in that way
☐ I will leave if people are not kind to me or I feel ashamed
☐ I will not let anyone shame me
☐ I will not be open to feedback, especially in public

in order to *(in no particular order, and add your own)* . . .

- be safe from shame and humiliation
- keep myself from doing violence
- not make mistakes
- belong to my parents and family
- _____
- _____
- _____

no matter the cost to myself or those I love.

**EXERCISE** **Releasing Privilege-Related Unconscious Contracts**

I, <u>(YOUR NAME HERE)</u>, promise myself that I will:
*(Insert the Contract Beginnings that you find true for yourself here, as you identified earlier in the questionnaire "Which Contracts Try to Help Us Survive White Fragility?")*

_____

_____

_____

Then follow the "General Worksheet to Release Unconscious Contracts" to release any of the contracts that feel true to you.

**IN CLOSING**

**The Importance of Humility**

We've learned that white supremacy culture is designed for white people to have more privileges than people of other racial, cultural, and ethnic groups. Whiteness continues to determine how much freedom, resources, and opportunities we have access to. We also learned how easy it is for brains to be impacted by their proximity to power, and the difficulty for brains to see larger systems when they are navigating the double-binds of white supremacy culture.

In learning all of this, we may be moving out of this chapter with greater humility. This quality is exactly what is needed as we explore our capacity for antiracism with self-compassion, warm curiosity, the willingness to persist, and a strong sense of agency and community. It is important for us to feel this agency—to feel able to direct and fuel our choices. In Chapter 5 we learn about another automatic reaction human brains have that can complicate antiracist efforts: implicit bias.

# 5

# Bias, Disgust, and Coded Language

ANTIRACISM CONCEPT
## Cognitive Bias

Human brains and bodies together comprise the world's most complex supercomputer. As we navigate our world, we take in vast amounts of data, analyze it, use it as input into a series of algorithms and output the resulting thoughts, behaviors, and actions. Artificial intelligence famously produces racially biased results—from Facebook and Google's software classifying Black people as primates to erroneously identifying a Black man as a shoplifter, leading to his arrest and arraignment.[27] Our brains, just like computer algorithms, produce biased results. In order to handle the massive amount of data we take in, our brains create rules, or heuristics, that provide shortcuts in our decision-making. If we have access to complete and accurate information, we can make an optimal decision. Using heuristics, we make a decision that is based on partial information. The gap between the optimal decision and the one we make with partial information represents our cognitive bias.

Cognitive bias occurs in two ways. Either the data that we take in is limited or the rule we use to evaluate the data we do take in and determine a course of action with is flawed. White supremacy culture contributes to bias by affecting both pathways. We take in false or incomplete ideas about people, ideas governed by white supremacy culture. Repeated ideas and stories about a group, even when false, become part of the data available to our brains to make decisions. When I, Roxy, was a child, my parents noted how crime news included photos or mentioned race when the arrested person was Black or Latine, but rarely did so if they were white. Frequent exposure to stories of Black/Latine folks as criminals input that pairing as data into the brains of millions of people watching the news.

We also learn rules, either explicitly given to us or implicitly, as machine learning algorithms do, through enculturation and analysis of data. Rules like "Black people are criminals" can be explicitly stated or implicitly learned, then applied in our decisions. To determine if the person approaching us is safe, we use the rules as shortcuts to minimize the effort of data-gathering. Instead of looking for behavioral signs of danger (Are they holding a weapon? Is their face contorted with rage?), we use the rule "Black people are criminals, this person is Black, therefore they are more likely to be a criminal and dangerous." If the person is not Black, since we are unlikely to have a rule about their group being criminals, we look for more data to influence our decision.

While flawed heuristics can lead us to make decisions without gathering necessary information, cognitive bias can also lead to problems with the data we gather. It can affect how we perceive the world around us, what information we attend to and what we ignore. I described how judgments could be made about Black people's dangerousness without any supporting data. However, even information that is ostensibly gathered can be perceived inaccurately. Several news reports describe police shooting Black men because they mistakenly identified objects the men were holding as guns (e.g., phone, wallet, vape pen) and concluded they were under attack.[28]

Researchers have identified many types of bias that influence our

decision-making. Several types of bias are especially relevant in helping us understand how our brains' propensity to take shortcuts contributes to and reinforces existing racial bias. This is but one of the
complex mix of elements that drives racist behavior.

## Representative Heuristic

**We tend to believe things are true that are congruent with the rules
or models we have already learned or acquired.**

Here's an apocryphal example that will be used to illustrate various
types of bias. Two friends, one Black and one white, walk separately
into a store, working together to shoplift. The store's security guard
has a mental model of what a shoplifter looks like: Black youth. As
the teenagers browse the store, the guard notices they both pick up
items, look around, and put them back down. The guard decides
the Black teenager's behavior is suspicious because it matches the
guard's mental model. As the guard follows the Black teenager, the
white youth takes advantage of the guard's focus on the Black youth,
shoplifts, and departs the store.

## Confirmation Bias

**We tend to look for, attend to, and believe information that is
congruent with our preexisting beliefs.**

In the same example, the guard pays attention to specific information—the Black teenager is wearing an oversized hoodie and baggy
jeans, and is carrying a large backpack. The guard pays attention to
the information that confirms the "Blacks as shoplifters who should
be watched" belief, and ignores other information, such as the logo
on the teenager's sweatshirt that suggests the teen is on the fencing
team at the expensive private school in the neighborhood.

## Illusory Truth Effect

**Repetitive information is accepted as truth.**

The security guard likely received multiple iterations of the message that Black people shoplift. Taking in this message from multiple sources—fellow security guards, news, social media, TV shows, and so forth—the guard accepts it as truth. Research shows this is not true—Black, Latine, and white people shoplift at the same rate.[29]

## Group Attribution Error

**We conclude an individual's behavior is representative of everyone in their group.**

We may see this error in action if the security guard in our example caught a Black person shoplifting in the past and now assumes because that person shoplifted *all* Black people shoplift.

## Availability Bias

**The more easily we remember a past event, the more likely we are to think it will happen again.**

One way this might work is the guard has caught numerous people shoplifting in the past, white and Black. Most of the time, the same thing happens—the guard intervenes, the shoplifter either leaves the item, or the police come and arrest the shoplifter. One time the guard arrested a Black person just as the guard's favorite celebrity entered the store. The guard was starstruck. When the guard thinks of shoplifters, their first memory is of the time they caught that Black youth shoplifting when the A-lister walked into the store. With this memory easily accessible, the guard thinks, *I remember a Black kid shoplifting that time. I bet this Black kid is going to try the same thing now.*

## Headwind/Tailwind Bias

**We remember challenges we faced more readily than support we've received.**

When the guard tries to stop the Black youth from leaving the store, some adults in the store confront the guard, accusing the guard of racial profiling. The guard pushes past them and discovers some other adults at the door had stopped the youth from leaving and were waiting for the security guard to arrive. The guard, in telling what happens, recalls only the headwind—*I was trying to stop that kid from shoplifting and all these people tried to block me.* The guard doesn't mention the help they received.

## In-Group Bias

**We prefer people like us and support them more than those we think are dissimilar.**

The white security guard has discretion on how to respond after stopping youth who are shoplifting. The guard tends to make white youth return the product they are stealing, takes their name, and sends them home. The guard warns them: "You don't want to do this, you got your whole future ahead of you." The guard tends to call the police and press charges when Black youth shoplift.

Racist systems, beliefs, and behaviors contribute to bias, which in turn reinforces those racist beliefs and behaviors. In the example of the security guard and the shoplifters, we can see how different forms of bias can interact with and reinforce each other. Some people worry that if we accept cognitive bias as part of being human, people might assume they have a pass to be racist: "I just can't help it. I don't want to stereotype, but this is how my brain works." It's exactly the opposite. Begin by accepting that bias exists but recognize that unlike computers we can choose to moderate the impact of the racist information we consume and make antiracist choices. We can do so by continuously challenging the racist beliefs that fuel bias and, before acting, pause to question the assumptions driving our actions.

Scientist Jessica Nordell writes in the conclusion of her in-depth exploration of how to end bias:

> We can begin noticing our own biased reactions, which are often so habitual they are difficult to see. Once seen, they can be questioned and interrupted. We can practice mindful awareness to help observe these reactions more clearly and better regulate our internal landscape....We can form meaningful, collaborative connections with people unlike ourselves; in doing so, we can increase the complexity with which we see others. Further, we can build structured decision-making into our institutions and organizations to reduce the role of bias in everyday practices.[30]

 JOURNALING PROMPT
**Acknowledging Our Cognitive Bias**

We are all subject to the information-processing limitations of human brains. We all evidence bias. Identify a time when you have enacted a racially biased response to someone. Write about what happened. Review the descriptions of the types of bias described in this chapter. How do you see those biases impacting your behavior? What feelings and needs arise now as you explore how cognitive bias shows up in your life?

_____

_____

_____

_____

_____

NEUROSCIENCE CONCEPTS
## Disgust and Coded Words

*From Sarah:*

I knew that our brains create patterns, but I didn't realize that we don't get to choose the patterns our brains make. The phrase for this is "implicit bias": when our brains unconsciously create patterns about other people, based on what's visible about them and the values society has assigned to those qualities (i.e., skin color, class/caste, native language, clothing, etc.). We pick these up from family, from community, from media. All humans have them. It is how our brains work: they make patterns, and we could not live without them. But when the patterns subconsciously encode harmful stereotypes about large groups of people who look or sound like each other, they damage immune systems and health levels (as we explore in Chapter 8 on microaggressions).

The research of Jennifer Eberhardt of Stanford University shows these unknown-to-us beliefs affect us at the level of even whether we can recognize one another across races; if we're told that a person is a certain race, we will draw them differently, even if the original look of the person is undefined.[31] One of the things to watch out for with implicit bias is the ease with which we can be manipulated by social disgust and by fear. If we leave our disgust unexamined, politicians can manipulate it by using words that invoke it—terms like "welfare queen" or "drug lord." When words and phrases are said that have been linked with a particular skin color—*boom!*—the whole disgust and fear apparatus that has been waiting to be activated within us springs into action. And we do whatever it is that the politician or preacher or newscaster wants us to do—elect politicians to fund the drug war, make abortions illegal, limit voting rights for people of color, discontinue funding and health care for hungry families.

Or worse, we join white nationalist groups that bring violence against other humans, or we fail to notice redlining (the discriminatory practice in the United States that consists of a systematic policy, enforced by governmental regulations in writing, of denial of such services as mortgages, insurance, and other financial services to residents of certain areas, based on their race or ethnicity). Redlining prevented African American families from owning properties and from maintaining or improving them if they did own them, which prevented them from building intergenerational wealth, unlike their white counterparts who did. Gentrification, now happening worldwide, is a related process in which affordable housing is purchased by wealthy individuals. The area becomes unaffordable to people without economic privilege; neighborhoods and communities are destroyed.

QUESTIONNAIRE
## What Do Coded Words Do to You?

What racial groups do you think of when you hear these coded terms, and do you feel either fear or disgust? If you feel neither, don't put any checks in the third column.

| CODED TERM | RACIAL GROUP | FEAR OR DISGUST |
|---|---|---|
| Migrant worker | _____ | ☐ |
| Urban | _____ | ☐ |
| Uppity | _____ | ☐ |
| Inner city | _____ | ☐ |
| Bad neighborhood | _____ | ☐ |
| Risky neighborhood | _____ | ☐ |
| Dangerous neighborhood | _____ | ☐ |
| Projects | _____ | ☐ |
| Sassy | _____ | ☐ |
| Unemployed | _____ | ☐ |
| Poor | _____ | ☐ |
| Bossy | _____ | ☐ |
| Welfare | _____ | ☐ |

Terrorist _____ ☐
Illegal immigrant _____ ☐
Baby mama _____ ☐
Thug _____ ☐
Drug war _____ ☐

 **JOURNALING PROMPT**
**Coded Words**

Take a moment to consider all the ways that you have been unknowingly manipulated by the use of these words. What have you been tempted to think? Who have you been tempted to root for? How have these words blocked your solidarity with other groups of people? Who have you been tempted to condemn? How have these words prevented you from looking at the larger systemic problems in your own country?

_____

_____

_____

_____

_____

_____

The more interpersonal disgust we have (e.g., feeling disgust about sitting in someone else's seat if it's still warm, wearing a stranger's clothes, etc.), the more negative our attitudes are toward immigrants, foreigners, and "socially deviant" groups.[32] Although many emotions change with understanding and resonance, the emotions of contempt and disgust are more fixed and don't shift as easily in response to being understood. In order to work with these emotions, we need to find out what lies beneath them—often, but not always, it is grief or fear.

## Losing Self-Compassion When We Learn about Implicit Biases

As humans we have a biological imperative to be able to have full control over ourselves and our world, even though that is neurobiologically impossible. We like to imagine that we are the masters of our own brains and that we make our own choices. As we learn about implicit biases and about the way politicians and the media can manipulate us by using our unconscious disgust, we can feel some helplessness, shame, and self-condemnation. To protect ourselves from these feelings that arise when we discover we are less in charge of our brains than we thought, we may (1) deny the research showing our lack of choice or (2) believe it but at the cost of our self-compassion and self-respect. Either of those responses will be particularly likely if we have unconscious contracts that we should be in control.

  QUESTIONNAIRE
### Do You Have Unconscious Control Contracts?

Give each item a number, 0–5 *(0 = not true at all, 5 = very true)*:

____ I am in control of my life.

____ I do not permit mistakes on my watch.

____ People fail because they are lazy and careless.

____ I rarely make mistakes.

____ I schedule my workdays carefully and am on time for meetings.

____ There is a place for everything, and everything is in its place.

____ I have trouble delegating.

____ I am very good at anticipating problems and preventing them.

____ It is hard for me to trust that others will be able to take care of themselves.

____ I don't trust that the world is safe.

____ **TOTAL**

SCORING:

**0–20:** You are probably not upset, ashamed, or in protest to learn about implicit bias. You may not have unconscious control contracts.

**21–34:** You probably feel a little bad about your brain doing things without your consent. It would be worth it to explore the unconscious contracts that leave you vulnerable to shame.

**35–50:** You probably find it disturbing that your brain makes conclusions about people outside of your awareness. It would be supportive for your learning about antiracism to let some of these control contracts go.

Now try to articulate some of your unconscious control contracts and use the "General Worksheet to Release Unconscious Contracts" to work through and release them.

### NEW SKILL
## Making Observations

In antiracism work, clear observations—that provide a window into each person's perception of reality—are essential since they help us recognize and question the effects of cognitive bias and manipulative language. We make observations to share what we experience and to understand another's experience. As we do so, we remember that we each see the world from a different location, so we hold our observation as *our* truth, not *the* truth. What we observe can be shaped by our past experience, the impact of cognitive bias, and our understanding of the context we live in. Making a detailed observation helps us gain clarity about what we are reacting to (Figure 2). The more nuanced and specific we can be about the stimulus that impacts us, the more we can understand that impact and find ways to address it.

## *Observation Iceberg*

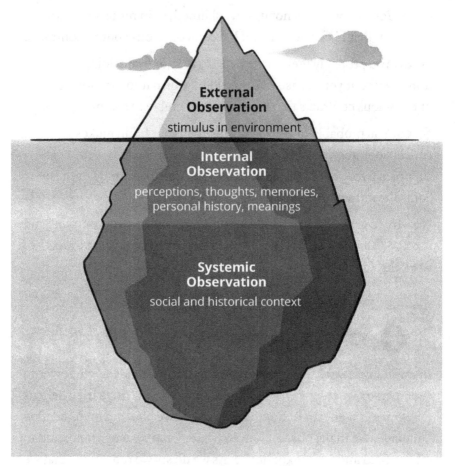

**FIGURE 2. Levels of Observations**
© Mireille van Bremen and Roxy Manning

### *Levels of Observations*

We can make observations on three levels.

**External observations** are the stimulus we perceive in the environment. This might be an object, someone's actions or words, someone's inaction. People are most likely to reach agreement about external observations. However, because cognitive bias affects even what we attend to, a person in the same setting might not notice the same behavior or action that we do. If you were to record the entire setting and share it with the person, you could point out what they missed. Roxy shares an external observation: "When I took the exit ramp off the highway, I switched lanes. A police car drove up behind me and turned on its lights, which usually indicates one should pull over."

**Internal observations** are our internal landscape. They include our awareness of our sensations in the moment, our memories and thoughts. We can never know another person's internal observation; they can share it with us. If someone does not share their internal observation, we maintain awareness that there is another level of stimuli that the person is experiencing that we do not know. If we attempt to make guesses about another person's internal observation, we should be cautious since this is one place where our cognitive biases might impact our guess of their internal experience. Roxy notes her internal observation when she was pulled over in a traffic stop: "My internal observation included feeling shaky and crying. Some memories were activated by the sight of the flashing lights in my mirror. Without consciously choosing to, I remembered being stopped on the street because I was suspected of robbing a store. I remembered stories of Black people who were arrested after being stopped for minor traffic violations."

**Systemic observations** are our understandings of the relevant social and historical context. They include our understanding of the policies and systems that shape society, the patterns of impact such as systemic racism, and our awareness of stereotypes and other beliefs that are held about different groups. *The Guardian* shared a systemic observation that applies to Roxy's situation: "Black drivers make up 28% of those killed in traffic stops, while accounting for only 13% of the population."[33] Systemic observations are both verifiable and, like all observations, can be influenced by cognitive bias. Especially as they involve statistics and patterns, systemic observations are vulnerable to errors of confirmation bias (*What am I choosing to measure, and what am I ignoring?*), availability heuristic (*What patterns do I remember, and what do I forget?*), and more.

With all three levels of observations, we hold curiosity about what observations someone might make as it helps us to understand their reaction to a stimulus, especially when the reaction is different than our own.

WORKSHEET

## Practice Making Observations

Let's first work with an experience Roxy had. This is the external observation:

> I am at a campus event where I am scheduled to lead a workshop
> with a white, cisgender, male colleague. We both stand behind
> the registration desk looking at our notes. At different times, three
> people approach me and ask for logistical help—for instance, can I
> get them a receipt, can I share where the preworkshop gathering is
> taking place, can I get them an extra copy of the packet for a col-
> league who will arrive late. One of them also asks if I can point out
> the trainer because they had a question about the content. No one
> approaches my colleague for help.

What do you guess Roxy's internal observations might be?

_____

_____

_____

_____

What are some systemic observations that could be made in this scenario? If you are stuck, what hidden messages about race might you imagine? What patterns in society give rise to that hidden message?

_____

_____

_____

_____

Now think of an example of bias that you experienced. You might have been the target, you might have committed it, or you might have observed it. Describe what happened. This is the external observation.

_____

_____

_____

_____

What was the internal observation?

_____

_____

_____

_____

What systemic observations can you make?

_____

_____

_____

_____

**IN CLOSING**
## The Remedy Is Learning

Learning about how politicians (and others who have power, such as media personalities and corporate media owners) have influenced our brains so that we feel what the powerholders want us to feel and learning about the role of implicit bias can generally be disheartening. However, in this chapter we have learned about some different forms of and remedies for unconscious bias. What we are learning here makes us more self-aware and increases our capacity to be intentional. We also learned about making observations at different levels and how this can help us to stay curious about other people's experiences, leading to increased understanding and possible connection.

With this knowledge and awareness we can be warmer, more relational (i.e., act from a sense of healthy interdependence), and more able to live and act in integrity with our longings for Beloved Community. In Chapter 6 we explore responding to harm and learn a model that helps us stay connected to the consciousness of nonviolence.

# 6

# Nonviolence:
# A Counter to Racism and Harm

 ANTIRACISM CONCEPT
**Responding to Harm**

Harm—what to do when it's directed at us, what to do when we learn our actions have resulted in it, what to do when we witness it happening—is challenging for many of us. Some of us freeze. "I can't believe this is happening to me," the Receiver might say. "I can't believe I just did that," the Actor might say. "I can't believe what I'm witnessing," the Bystander might say. Some of us leap into action with an urgency to stop the harm, no matter what. Action emerging from urgency without clarity often leads to people or needs being dropped. In antiracist work, reflecting ahead of time on how we want to respond to harm and what principles might guide our response can support us in responding quickly, but with clarity and intention, in the face of harm. In the next few chapters, we will explore separately some considerations for attending to harm for the Receiver, the Actor, and the Bystander. These considerations may be relevant for all of us, regardless of the role we occupy.

*Receiver*

When we receive harm from someone's actions, automatic responses might activate. We might freeze defensively—any response we make can result in even more harm, especially when the Actor has the power to levy consequences against us. We might attack. Some of us have learned that the way to prevent even more harm is to fight and drive away those whose actions harm us. We might seek to placate. We have learned that a submissive, fawning reaction can defuse the animus of the Actor and result in their stopping the harmful behavior. Conversely, we may have some urgency to respond. We might worry: *If I don't respond, am I sending a message that I'm okay with this? If I don't respond right when the harm happens, have I ceded any legitimacy to respond later? How can I send a clear message that this is not okay?*

As a Receiver, we first assess our immediate danger. What is the nature of the harm that is happening? Unless we intentionally put ourselves in harm's way to draw attention to an injustice, we likely want to stop the harm and ensure safety. Our first step is to assess what is needed to protect safety for ourselves and those present. Sometimes we may choose to leave the situation or to not risk censure or retaliation by filing a complaint or publicly protesting the harm. It is important to note that the choice to leave a harmful situation, even a physically harmful one, is not always available. Many people who find themselves in physically harmful situations experience constrained choice. An employee who is being physically harassed by staff and other managers may desperately want to leave, but their choice to do so is constrained by the lack of availability of jobs in the area and the employee's need for sustainability to feed and care for their family. In order to attend to harm, as a Receiver we must know what we are willing to risk—and for how long.

Next, pause and take stock of our options. Is it possible to leave the setting so that we have spaciousness to reflect and be intentional in our choice? Do we need support? If we have just experienced harm, our nervous system may be activated. We may need accompaniment and resonance in order to regulate ourselves before we can explore the needs that will inform our actions. As social beings, we often need each other's support to "come back to ourselves," to shift from our reactive minds to our intentional, grounded selves. Yet in a society that values independence, we may have deep-seated self-judgments about seeking support, and this basic act of turning to each other for help may feel like a big stretch.

One way to build our capacity for accessing support is to intentionally develop relationships within existing or new circles of community in which we have a practice of turning to each other when needing empathy or a space to think things through. For some of us this may be a relatively easy adaptation of a new practice explicitly added to our existing relationships. For others it may be a longer process of cultivating a new community of mutual care and support. Still, intentionally building, maintaining, and caring for a network of mutually supportive relationships is an essential source of help in addressing the impacts of harm. We, as human beings, were not designed to do this alone.

As a Receiver, next we identify both our immediate needs and our long-term goals. We try to connect to both the needs around the specific situation itself and to our long-term values and dreams. If we attend to the needs relevant to the current situation, what needs would be met in relation to our long-term goals, including the goal of contributing to Beloved Community, and what needs would go unmet? Holding awareness of all that is important to us, we choose a response that holds care for both our capacity and needs in the moment and also for our long-term goals.

The Authentic Dialogue framework's roots in the philosophy of nonviolence invite us to reconsider responding to harm with intentional violence. A dualistic perspective of good/bad implies that good is rewarded and bad is punished. Many of us have internalized that framework when it comes to antiracism work; we see it in the public shaming and calls for firing of people who are deemed "racist." Using principles of nonviolence, we aim instead to respond to harm with the least amount of force necessary to stop the harm. Nonviolent Communication practitioners often differentiate between protective and punitive use of force. When we seek to use just enough force to stop harm, then search for strategies to eliminate the repetition of harm while attending to the needs of both Receivers and Actors, we are choosing a protective use of force.

Once the harm has stopped, we don't use more force than necessary to prevent a return of the harm. If we use force when protection is no longer necessary, even with an intent to educate or inspire behavior change, the use of force is punitive. Strategies like exclusion and shaming may serve to stop some behavior, but they result in many unmet needs. These strategies contribute to the us-versus-them, good/bad binary and do not support us in coming together, uniting in the work of finding strategies that attempt to meet needs for all. As a Receiver, we might feel resistance to the idea of not just stopping harm but also seeking solutions that include the needs of those who have harmed.

Does this not reward bad behavior? It is the opposite. Protective use of force and inclusive strategies to attend to harm provide the greatest benefit for the Receiver. If we always include the needs of Beloved Community as essential in any solution we consider, then full care for the Receiver's needs must also include attending to the Actor's needs. Again, to only attend to the needs of the Receiver means we inadvertently submit to and reinforce the either/or punitive paradigm.

Conversely, when we attend to the needs of the Actor as well, we affirm their humanity at a moment in which they may be judging themselves and become driven to justify themselves at any cost. In attending to the Actor's needs, we eliminate their motivation to use costly strategies to get their needs met. In addition, when we attend to the needs of the person who finds themselves in the position of the Actor, we acknowledge that there have been and will be situations in which we will be Actors. Offering understanding and care to both the Receiver and the Actor, to the persons occupying these roles in a given situation, creates an environment in which everyone can trust when we take actions that others find painful, we too will be held with care. This is essential for sustaining truly Beloved Community.

Let's look at the example of Morgan, who demonstrated the power of acting from connection to all his needs rather than punitively. The only Black player on his sports team, Morgan received continuous disparaging comments from his coach. Mistakes other players made were ignored, but if made by Morgan resulted in Coach mocking him, calling him names, exaggeratingly mimicking his body movements. One day, Morgan left practice, tears of anger and despair streaming down his face. As he discussed his options, he identified his current needs. At that moment, Morgan wanted respect, kindness, and support. He was deeply confused and hurt, and he longed for acceptance and understanding. He yearned for acknowledgment and appreciation of his efforts.

Exhausted and hopeless, Morgan desperately wanted relief. He considered quitting the team or reporting Coach's behavior, but then also connected with his long-term needs. He knew reporting Coach would end that year's program because of the difficulty of finding a new coach so late in the season. Morgan became aware he wanted to maximize opportunities for learning and growth. Playing, even with Coach's disfavor, provided those chances. Quitting or reporting Coach would take those opportunities away from him. Morgan decided after connecting with his full array of needs to complete the season with Coach. He also arranged emotional support before and after practice.

This support enabled Morgan to stay grounded and connected to his needs; he was less reactive to Coach's continued abuse. He determined that when the season ended, he would report Coach's behavior. This would give those in charge time to figure how to address it or to find a new coach for the team without interrupting the current season. Trusting he could make the report a few months in the future, Morgan was able to focus on strategies that could help him and his teammates survive and harvest the growth he sought. Morgan did speak up after the season ended and a new coach was hired before the next season began.

Morgan's example is one option in which he continued to experience harm as he was unable to think of a way to meet his ultimate needs without doing so. He also may have chosen to leave the team (self-care), or organize other players to engage with administration (collective action). There is no one right answer—each person decides for themselves, if possible in collaboration with other Receivers, what strategies hold care for as many needs as possible.

In this example, those with power eventually chose a punitive strategy (firing the coach) rather than any other purely protective strategies (e.g., having a new head coach and retaining the current coach to work under that person, with clear requests for behavior changes and consistent monitoring and feedback). As Receivers who currently work within systems that might not share our values, we still raise awareness of issues and ask for support, and where we can, we let our opposition to punitive strategies be known. Like Morgan, we can use the consciousness and tools of Nonviolent Communication when we identify what is challenging to us in any situation to come to a strategy that truly supports us.

### NEW SKILL
### The OFNR Process

Nonviolent Communication combines the consciousness of nonviolence with a specific communication process—identifying observations, feelings, needs, and requests (often abbreviated as OFNR and pronounced "off-ner").[34] The OFNR process is a model that helps us stay connected to the consciousness of nonviolence that we value. The four steps of OFNR help us differentiate between the information we want to convey and that which can be barriers to connection. We differentiate observations from interpretations, feelings from thoughts, needs from strategies, and requests from coercive demands. Let's look at each of these four components.

*Observations*

We explored observations in Chapter 5, so we will not redefine them here. We want to highlight instead the differentiation between observations and interpretations. When we make observations, we report on what we are perceiving. This is especially true for external observations. When we share our perception, free from our interpretation, the listener gets a sense of what we are responding to. It is not presented as *the* truth but *our* truth, since we acknowledge that we each may perceive a different facet of the same event. When we share our internal observations, we are even more careful to report this as *our* experience, not a universal one. We can observe the thoughts or memories activated by the stimulus reported in the external observation. Sharing them will help the listener understand what we're reacting to, but it does not establish our internal observation as more true or less true than the listener's.

*Feelings*

When we share our feelings, we want to differentiate them from our thoughts. In English, as in many languages, we have words that are defined as feeling words but include our thoughts in them—Roxy calls these words fusion words. For instance, suppose a white supervisor agreed to support their Global Majority staff member during a presentation, then stayed silent while the staff member struggled while answering several tough questions. Afterward, the staff member told their supervisor: "I felt abandoned." A word like "abandoned" suggests the staff member's belief about what the supervisor did—"You did not step in to help me"—and that they had an emotional reaction to that action. If they use the word "abandoned," we don't actually know how they feel. Are they angry? Worried? Insecure? Confused? In addition, the supervisor might not agree with the implied thought part of that fusion word: "I didn't abandon you! You were handling it and I wanted to give you space to respond. I worried my stepping in would be seen as a white person rescuing and prevent people from seeing how capable you were. I was prepared to pause and check in if you needed it, but you always did fine."

Using a word that has a nonexplicit message about someone else's behavior embedded in it opens the door for the conversation to be sidelined by an argument about whether or not they agree with our thought, rather than focusing on connecting with our experience. By focusing on the feeling, OFNR aims to make it more likely that the emotional response we had to a stimulus is known. There are many, many fusion words. Don't treat them as bad! Instead, use them as a guide that can help us determine what is going on for us or the person using them. If the employee said, "You abandoned me," I would first check to see if I understood the observation they were pointing to: "It seems we had a different understanding of what would be supportive to you. Were you hoping I would redirect or even step in if the group seemed hostile?" Then I would guess the feeling: "Were you feeling anxious?" Take a moment to review the "Feelings" chart in the Appendix (Figure 5).

### Needs

We aim to separate our needs (aspects of life shared by all humans that motivate our behavior) from our strategies (actions we take to meet our needs). Making this distinction helps us to share what is important to us, what is the underlying driver of our reaction to stimulus. In the previous example, if the employee was needing support and protection, they might feel angry or worried that their supervisor did not step in. However, if they were eager for an opportunity for growth, they might feel relieved that their supervisor was available if needed and proud that they were able to respond effectively to a challenging situation without assistance. The effect of the same external observation (the supervisor watching while the employee struggled to respond to tough questions) is mediated by the person's needs and results in vastly different feelings.

When we share our needs with someone, we are sharing what is important to us. Another person may not believe that need is activated for them in *this* moment, but they can accept it is for us. Moreso, if what we share is truly a need, truly universal, it will be something the other person can recognize as important to them also—maybe not in the current moment but at some point in their life. Take a look at the "Needs and Values" chart in the Appendix (Figure 6).

In the employee example, even if we both have the same need—such as for support—when we discuss strategies, we can run into disconnection. For example, my preferred strategy is that you let me know you're available, then wait for me to ask when I want your support. Your favorite strategy when you want support is for me to ask you what you would like rather than wait for you to ask, and then you offer several suggestions on what I can do. Your strategy would not land as support for me—it requires more interaction than I want. My strategy would not land as support for you—it doesn't provide the sense of involvement and care that you enjoy. We might argue about the best strategy but would both continue to agree about the importance of the need—for support. Sharing our needs serves to create a pathway to Beloved Community, one paved in our common humanity rather than any preferences for one strategy or another.

### Requests

Once we are clear on our needs, we may want to take action to meet our needs. We think of the strategy that we believe would best meet our needs and ideally, the needs of all involved. When we make a request, we try to advocate for what is important to us while supporting choice for others. We differentiate requests from demands, which remove choice from the other person. When addressing enduring inequities, such as through antiracist work, Roxy finds it helpful to differentiate between coercive demands, which insist on specific strategies, with generative demands, which insist on attention to meeting the needs.

When we make coercive demands, we identify one strategy to meet our needs and insist on that strategy, no matter the potential cost. Some people are drawn to coercive demands especially when harm is high. They take an "ends justify means" stance. We might also find ourselves issuing coercive demands when we are unable to imagine other strategies could exist that would attend to our needs. Coercive demands, especially when we have the power to force others to comply with them, can result in our needs being met at great cost to the other person and often at the expense of our own values around building communities that allow everyone to thrive, not just those holding power to get their way.

With generative demands, we insist on the commitment of the time and energy necessary to create effective strategies to attend to unmet needs. A generative demand is like refusing to get up from the negotiating table until a path forward is agreed to. It isn't an insistence on "my way or the highway"—instead, it's a persistence that demands engagement (even, if necessary, through nonviolent direct action) in creating a strategy to address long-unmet needs. Often, the needs that have been unmet or ignored the longest are those of members of the Global Majority and others who face structural barriers to equity. These can include everything from basic survival needs to the needs for respect and having a say in one's own future. Holding these needs firmly while maintaining flexibility in how to meet the needs (openness to requests for specific strategies or solutions) can produce generative energy for change.

WORKSHEET **Identify OFNR from a Description of a Difficult Situation**

Think of a time when you felt angry. The anger may be in response to something a person did, or it might be a response to the application of an inequitable rule or policy.

*Identify the Observation*

Write down what happened (refer to Figure 2 for guidance).

What was the external observation?

_____

_____

_____

What was your internal observation?

_____

_____

_____

What was the systemic observation?

_____

_____

_____

*Connect with Your Feelings*

As you read each of your observations, what feelings do you notice? If you are not able to connect with your feelings, think about the situation and notice your body sensations. While doing so, scan the

"Feelings" chart in the Appendix (Figure 5) to see what words your body responds to. Write down the feelings you identify.

_____

_____

_____

### Identify the Needs

What is important to you as you consider the situation? What needs can you identify? If you cannot articulate your needs, again, consider the situation and the feelings you identified. Choose an observation and the feeling that was connected to it. Complete the sentence:

"When _____ *(name the observation)*, I felt _____ *(name the feeling)* because _____ *(scan the needs list and choose one your body responds to)* was important to me.

Write down the needs you identified.

_____

_____

_____

### Formulate a Request

What is an action you or another person could take that could contribute to one of the needs you described being met? Who is the person? What is the thing they can do? Be as specific as possible. Be careful to think of what you want them to *do*, not what you want them to *stop doing*. When would you like them to do it by? Write down the full request, including the who, what, and when.

_____

_____

_____

Now put these together into one OFNR statement by choosing an observation and filling in the blanks with the elements you identified earlier that are connected to that statement.

When _____,
        *(write one observation from any level)*

I felt _____
        *(write a feeling word you identified connected to that observation)*

because I need/value _____.
        *(write a need connected to that feeling)*

Would you consider _____?
        *(write the request that would meet the need above)*

 IN CLOSING **Staying Connected to the Consciousness of Nonviolence**

In this chapter we learned how to use the four steps of the Nonviolent Communication OFNR process to help us access the knowledge contained in our habitual reactions to harms that we experience or witness. These steps help to keep us anchored in the consciousness that can create Beloved Community, connected to the needs we are so longing for fulfillment of in the world. In Chapter 7 we explore how to define goals based on this self-knowledge to engage the Authentic Dialogue process.

# 7

# Moving into Authentic Dialogue

ANTIRACISM CONCEPT
**Authentic Dialogue**

Authentic Dialogue is a way of connecting that prioritizes transparent communication about challenges with the goal of arriving at solutions grounded in our values of inclusion, care for all, and our collective liberation. Using the Authentic Dialogue Framework (Figure 3), as fully developed by Roxy in the companion book *How to Have Antiracist Conversations*, we begin with the inner work necessary to understand and communicate our experience, with as little judgment or interpretation as possible.[35] As we connect to our shared needs, we are better able to understand our reactions in the moment, identify what is still important to us, and choose whether and how we want to communicate with another person. The triple clarity of intention, self-knowledge, and purpose supports us as we select and enter this type of communication.

NEW SKILL **Clarifying Goals and Choosing the Authentic Dialogue**

Often, when we become clear about our anger, we are ready to do something about it! We want people to get what we're angry about.

We feel compelled to stop the harm, relieve the pain, and fix the issue. Driven by the intensity of our emotions and an urgency to see change, we leap into a dialogue. However, without more clarity on our specific goals for the dialogue, we risk ending that dialogue still angry, still dissatisfied. To maximize the chance that our dialogue can have the hoped-for productive impact, we need to do some work before beginning one. It may seem obvious, but the most important pre-dialogue step to take is to understand *why* we want to have the dialogue. My anger might signal a need for a dialogue, but it doesn't give me clarity about the purpose of the dialogue. In the Authentic Dialogue framework we identify four distinct purposes underlying each of the main dialogues.

### Dialogue to Be Heard

Within every request for a dialogue, no matter the purpose, is a request to be heard. If we as Receivers seek a Dialogue to Be Heard, we want to share our experience and receive reflections that demonstrate what is important to us was understood by the listener. We may not want anything else to happen in the moment. Sometimes it's enough to know that finally our pain, our anger, the depth of our experience was received. We may not have the capacity to listen to the other person ourselves, and we may not be ready to move to working on a solution. If we suspect that is the case, we can let those constraints be known when requesting a Dialogue to Be Heard. This enables the listener in the dialogue to decide if they can agree to listen without being heard.

If the listener is a Bystander, then listening to the Receiver with no expectation to share might not be a challenge. If the listener is the Actor or a Bystander who wants to be heard, agreeing to partake in a unidirectional Dialogue to Be Heard as a listener does not mean they will never have a chance to share their experience. There can be separate listening sessions, each focused on a specific speaker. Or someone else can be the listener for the Bystander or the Actor. The

## Authentic Dialogue Framework

## Preparation

*Consciousness:*

- Affirm the commitment to Beloved Community as the ultimate goal guiding each step of this dialogue.
- Remember all human behavior is motivated by needs.
- Acknowledge the existence of white supremacy thinking and other forms of oppression.
- Aim for solutions that advance our collective liberation.

*Inner Work:*

- Clarify what happened. What is the external observation?
- Surface any thoughts or judgments.
- Ask what might have been missed. Are cognitive biases impacting perception?
- Identify the internal observation. What memories and experiences were triggered?
- Determine what systemic observations were stimulated.
- Scan your body and identify sensations and emotions.
- Self-empathize to gain clarity on needs.
- Identify your purpose in asking for a dialogue.
- Determine what risk you are willing to accept balancing your needs and your intention to move toward Beloved Community.
- Identify barriers to dialogue.

## Core Dialogue

*Dialogue*
***to Be Heard***

- Use connection requests in every element of the dialogue.
- Make the ask: Check willingness for dialogue.
- Make agreements to attend to any barriers that exist.
- Determine together if everyone will be heard. If more than one person will share, determine who shares first.
- Listening Steps:
    - Reflect the person's experience.
    - Empathize with all levels of impact.
    - Acknowledge systemic contributions.

## Expanded Dialogues

*Dialogue for Healing*

- Begin with a **Dialogue to Be Heard.**
- Give space for Receiver to connect with and express emotional impact and be received with deep empathy.
- Identify any meaning and unconscious contracts that the Receiver holds in relation to the act.
- If Receiver is willing, consider possible needs motivating the Actor's action.
- Mourn unmet needs.
- Ensure each participant seeking healing is the focus of the listening steps.
- If clarity emerges that an action is desired, move to Dialogue for Solution.

*Dialogue for Shared Understanding*

- Begin with a **Dialogue to Be Heard**.
- Mourn unmet needs.
- Ensure each participant has an opportunity to express their experience and receive empathy.
- If clarity emerges that an action is desired, move to Dialogue for Solution.

*Dialogue for Solution*

- Begin with a **Dialogue to Be Heard.**
- Ensure each impacted person has an opportunity to express their needs.
- Summarize all needs identified.
- Brainstorm strategies to attend to as many needs as possible.
- Generate solution requests.
- Select solution prioritizing attending to as many needs as possible, including needs around equity.
- Agree on implementation timeline.
- Make agreements about follow-up.

FIGURE 3. **Authentic Dialogue Framework**
© Mireille van Bremen and Roxy Manning

Dialogue to Be Heard is the Core Dialogue of the Authentic Dialogue framework. It is the foundation, the beginning, of each of the other three dialogues.

### Dialogue for Shared Understanding

In a Dialogue for Shared Understanding, each person involved is clear that they wish to share their experience until mutual understanding of each person's perspective and what they value is achieved. In choosing this dialogue, everyone is clear that they have the desire and capacity to try and hear another's perspective with empathy and curiosity. Each person seeks to listen without defensiveness to the other. The aim is to make clear to everyone the different observations at each level that stimulated each person's experience and to see where there is congruence. We aim to bear witness to the array of needs that each person is longing to meet. A Dialogue for Shared Understanding may help us learn where information is missing that is necessary to have before proceeding to a Dialogue for Solution.

### Dialogue for Healing

We might request a Dialogue for Healing because we are seeking relief from the pain or judgments we are holding about a situation. In a Dialogue for Healing, we share our experience and full observation of the elements that are stimulating to us. We want to know that our experience, as the Receiver, matters. From that place we start with being heard fully for our experience, both what our perceptions of the observations were as well as the meaning we're making of it. We intend, in a Dialogue for Healing, to vulnerably reveal the full range of our experience and be empathically received. We experience healing when our vulnerability is matched by a depth and open-heartedness in those hearing us.

We also want to gain some insight into the needs that motivated the Actor to do the things that we find stimulating. When the Receiver has the experience of being deeply heard, we often organically experience a shift and readiness to understand the Actor's needs. Doing so can help us shift any narrative we may hold that what happened was our fault because we were somehow bad or that it happened because the Actor is bad. Moving away from those narratives is very healing. We seek to understand the needs in order to shift away from a moralistic judgment (the absolute good/bad binary evaluation). Instead, we aim to gain information about the needs that are motivating behavior, even behavior that was painful for us. Shifting from moralistic judgments helps us to see the Actor's full humanity, a step that is key to the goal of Beloved Community.

*Dialogue for Solution*

In a Dialogue for Solution we want to build on the foundational Dialogue to Be Heard. We are interested in finding ways to address unmet needs or harm that has occurred. We focus on gaining enough understanding of each person's needs in order to generate possible strategies that take into account all the needs. However, a Dialogue for Solution might limit the depth of empathy, aiming for sufficient understanding to support decision-making rather than healing.

You may not have realized it, but you have already begun practicing the foundational skills to participate in Authentic Dialogue. Before we begin the dialogue, we reflect on the elements of the Consciousness of Authentic Dialogue (Figure 3), which we use to ground us as we move through the dialogue. If you would like to review these elements before beginning a dialogue, here are a few places to get started:

### The commitment to Beloved Community

- Questionnaire: "Do I Actually Want Beloved Community?"
- Exercise: "Release the Contracts That Prevent the Intention to Live in Beloved Community"

### Understanding needs as the motivation for human behavior

- Worksheet: "From Violence to Nonviolence"
- New Skill: "The OFNR Process—Needs"

### The existence of white supremacy culture

- Journal: "You and White Supremacy Culture"
- Journal: "Reflecting on Privilege"

### Choosing strategies for collective liberation

- Journal: "Acknowledging Our Cognitive Bias"
- New Skill: "Making Observations"
- New Skill: "The OFNR Process—Requests"

We next do some preparation before beginning the dialogue. This preparation can help us have clarity about what stimulated us and what needs we have in relation to it. We also can explore which dialogue would support the needs we have identified. Think of the situation about which you'd like to request a dialogue. Then, use these worksheets to support you as you move through the Inner Work steps of the Authentic Dialogue Framework (Figure 3):

- Worksheet: "Practice Making Observations"
- Worksheet: "Identify OFNR from a Description of a Difficult Situation"

Once you complete those worksheets, you are ready to explore choosing a dialogue.

**WORKSHEET**
## Choosing a Dialogue

As you answer each question, follow the suggested exploration. You may finish it in one sitting or take several attempts to do so. Before choosing a suggested dialogue, read through the remaining questions to determine if you want to consider the explorations for a different type of dialogue.

1. What is important to you in this situation? What needs are you trying to meet with the dialogue?

_____

_____

_____

_____

_____

_____

If you don't already know your needs, do this self-empathy process: Think about your situation, notice your body sensations, and look at the "Needs and Values" chart in the Appendix (Figure 6) to see which needs your body responds to. Write those needs on the lines above. If you still are not clear, ask a friend to listen to you talk about the situation and reflect what they hear as being most important to you.

2. Ask yourself: "Do I worry that I will not be understood if I attempt a dialogue? Am I concerned that I cannot hold my own needs and choose authenticity given the other person's patterns of relating and expected levels of reactivity?"

☐ Yes      ☐ No

*(If "no," continue to the next question.)*

*(If "yes," consider what needs would be met for you if the dialogue was facilitated, and what qualities you would seek in a facilitator. Consider if you would benefit from having a support person present.)*

If you want more support, do a self-empathy process or seek empathy from another person (ask them to reflect their understanding of your feelings and needs) as you explore this question before continuing with this worksheet.

3. Are you experiencing sufficient pain, anger, or distrust that you are unable to hear the other person with curiosity and openness?

☐ Yes      ☐ No

*(If "no," continue to the next question.)*

*(If "yes," do you want to take this to the other person concerned in the experience?)*

If you want to take this to the person concerned, ask them for a Dialogue to be Heard or a Dialogue for Healing.

If you are not clear, seek empathy from another person before returning to this worksheet.

4. Do you have the clarity you seek on all the factors that are contributing to the situation?

☐ Yes      ☐ No

*(If "yes," continue to the next question.)*

*(If "no," if you want more support, do a self-empathy process or seek empathy from another person before returning to this worksheet.)*

If you are ready to connect, request a Dialogue for Shared Understanding.

5. Is there immediate harm occurring that you want to address?

☐ Yes      ☐ No

*(If "no," continue to the next question.)*

*(If "yes," clarify the nature of the harm that is happening and who is experiencing harm. This will enable you to be specific in your requests.)*

Once the harm is clarified, request a Dialogue for Solution focused on addressing the immediate harm. Once an agreement has been met, you can explore if a fuller dialogue is needed to address other unmet needs.

6. Am I interested in finding strategies that attend to the needs of all involved?

☐ Yes    ☐ No

*(If "yes," continue to the next question.)*

*(If "no," use empathy to explore if worry about scarcity, fear, judgments, or anger is getting in the way. Return to questions 2–4 to see if further explorations in these areas are necessary.)*

7. Consider an expanded Dialogue for Shared Understanding that can help you connect more fully with all the needs present.

Finally, move to a Dialogue for a Solution.

NEUROSCIENCE CONCEPT
## Secure Attachment and Repairs

Another part of the inner work of preparing for Authentic Dialogue is to better understand our own reactions to stress through recognizing and healing our attachment styles. "Secure attachment" means that we are connected enough to the people who are important to us, and to ourselves, that we can lean into our supportive relationships to get through difficult situations without acute stress. "Insecure attachment" means we have not had those supportive relationships. It means that we have to push ourselves along, using our own cortisol and our own stress response; repairs are more difficult and life more stressful.

There are three types of insecure attachment:

- **Avoidant attachment,** where we depend primarily on ourselves. When losing an argument or hearing that they've had a negative impact on someone else, this person tends to act like it didn't happen, to blame others, or to blame themselves.

- **Ambivalent (anxious) attachment,** where our functioning is dependent on how our relationships are going. When losing an argument or hearing that they've had a negative impact on someone else, this person tends to collapse in shame, to fight, or to obsessively try to reestablish contact.

- **Disorganized (traumatic) attachment,** where we respond unpredictably, with extreme emotions or dissociation, to difficult situations. When losing an argument or hearing that they've had a negative impact on someone else, this person tends to respond unpredictably, sometimes with humility and charm, sometimes with violence or a retreat into addiction.

We have these attachment styles with ourselves, with our parents and children, our partners, our companion animals, our spiritual teachers or deities (called a variety of names—for example, "God/Goddess," "Allah," "Yhwh," "Higher Power," and many more), and with concepts like antiracism.

From the standpoints of having privilege and not having privilege, here is what our attachment styles with antiracism look like. As you read through these differentiations, remember that we all, no matter our attachment styles, live in societies that are structured to make it possible to pretend that racism is the only way of living, that nothing can be changed, and that it is only adversely impacting Global Majority folks.

**Securely attached when we don't have privilege.** We are clear in who we are and know the importance of accompaniment and community.

We refuse definition by the white supremacy culture, while seeing what the big picture is and mourning the horrors of inequity in our systems. We take antiracist action in ways that are effective but not all-consuming. We become curious about what makes others make the choices that they do, and about the needs people are meeting with choices that we don't agree with. We stand strong in our own truth and receive enough support to continue to call for Beloved Community. We hold Beloved Community as a value that guides us into fierce and loving expression and action.

**Securely attached with privilege.** We are warmly curious about what others' experiences are, and we have the capacity to learn about the big picture and mourn the horrors of inequity in our systems. We take antiracist action in ways that are effective but not all-consuming. Once we learn that the social system that we live in is racist and why, we seek out information that will help us understand and change our system. We acknowledge our privilege while remaining humble and taking actions to change the dominant system. When we receive feedback about how we have negatively impacted others, we are able to mourn our missteps, learn from them, and make repairs when possible. When it is not possible to make repairs or for repairs to be made, we mourn and continue to be present to ourselves and others. We hold Beloved Community as a value that guides us into fierce and loving expression and action.

**Avoidantly attached without privilege.** We believe that life is bad, it's always been bad, it's never going to change, and that it's been this way forever. We construct our lives so that we can avoid contact with people or situations where we would have to confront racist situations. This is an avoidant way to take care of ourselves when we don't have privilege. We insulate ourselves for protection, physical safety, and to reduce stress. We avoid the dangers of fighting systemic racism and focus on trying harder and accomplishing more. Or we commit to consistently overachieving and to always being our best self to compensate for racism, taking all responsibility onto ourselves and not looking at the big picture. We "work three times as hard as a white person" and admonish our children to do the same.

**Avoidantly attached with privilege.** We don't think much about others' needs or experience, and we pay attention to our own goals and lives rather than to the big picture. We don't think about the systemic, because no matter how much we have, we're only thinking about the individual, and we're focused on beating scarcity. If we stumble across any information about systemic inequality, we change the channel so that we don't have to know. We construct our lives so that we can minimize or avoid contact with people or situations where we would have to acknowledge racism, or discuss racism, or learn about microaggressions or racism. We call all invitations to more consciousness "cancel culture" and classify discussions of inequality as hostile or blaming. We believe that inequity is just a part of life, and we don't have the sense that anything needs to be changed. When we receive feedback about how we have negatively impacted others, we feel annoyed or dismissive or completely mystified. We are hypervigilant to the way words are being used and to any hint that others are blaming us. We blame others rather than taking responsibility ourselves. It never even occurs to us to make repairs.

**Ambivalently attached without privilege.** Activism and challenging racism can be our whole identity. And/or we can find ourselves forever overextending and in shame. We are never working hard enough, and it is our responsibility to find some way to save everyone who is being harmed. We are either constantly stressed, or we become burned out and cannot participate at all because we have collapsed. It can be hard to recover from exhaustion with the relentless pile-up of racist violence.

**Ambivalently attached with privilege.** We are overwhelmed by others' experience, so we alternately drown in despair about systemic racism or try not to think about it. The big picture is too depressing, so we do the same thing. We throw ourselves into antiracist action to the point of burnout, and then we turn away from action altogether. We become anxious about our privilege, going so far as to ask a Global Majority friend to absolve us of our racial slips or sins. When we receive feedback about how we have negatively impacted others, we drown in shame and find it difficult to recover. We either can't imagine making a repair, or we can't believe the other person when they gracefully receive the attempt at repair. Whether or not it is possible to make repairs, we carry the shame until we move out of ambivalent attachment into earned secure attachment (discussed later) and we begin to heal.

**Disorganizedly attached with and without privilege.** Our response to antiracism is unpredictable. We can take on issues with great charisma, understanding, and leadership, while simultaneously behaving without integrity with people who have less power than we have. We can turn away from the issues and dissociate. We can join racist groups and support legislation that is inherently systemically racist. We can join antiracist groups that are committed to violence. When we receive feedback about how we have negatively impacted others, we can respond with beauty and grace, or with hatred and contempt.

**JOURNALING PROMPT**
## Attachment Styles

As you review the ways that our attachment styles can be reflected in our attitudes toward antiracism as discussed, which of the attitudes comes closest to your own experience?

_____

_____

_____

_____

_____

_____

We often believe our attachment style is permanent or "just the way we are," instead of seeing the possibility of moving toward secure attachment (the easiest way to be in relationship) with every contract we release and step toward healing that we take. When we move toward secure attachment, we become more responsive and resilient. This helps us to make repairs for negative impact on others, which moves everyone toward secure attachment.

**QUESTIONNAIRE**
## Discover Your Blocks to Self-Compassion

Each of these statements leads people to believe that if they make a mistake or impact someone else negatively, they lose their worth and their belonging. In antiracism work, as in all of life, it's important to be able to learn from mistakes and not have them destroy us or make us think we no longer belong.

Place check marks beside the statements that seem true to you.

☐ People don't change.

☐ You can't teach an old dog new tricks.

☐ I am what I am, and I just need to accept it.

☐ I am flawed and the best thing is to not think about it.

☐ I must never make mistakes.

☐ If I make a mistake I can never be forgiven/will lose my belonging.

☐ People who hurt other people shouldn't get to be part of the group.

☐ If I do harm, I can never be forgiven/will lose my belonging.

☐ If someone has hurt someone else, they did it on purpose.

☐ If someone doesn't really mean to hurt someone else, it makes it less harmful.

Which statement is most powerful for you?

For me, Sarah, today, the statement "If someone doesn't really mean to hurt someone else, it makes it less harmful" is most powerful. If I do the following exercise, it sounds like this: "I, Sarah, promise myself that I will believe that if I don't really mean to hurt someone else, it makes it less harmful. I will believe this in order to preserve my innocence and my own sense of worth and mitigate the harm that I can't help doing as a part of this system of social inequality, no matter the cost to myself and the people I love." The cost is that if someone tells me that I hurt them, I start defending myself by telling them my intentions, instead of actually listening to them, and so I can't learn from the impact my actions have had. Do I like this promise? No. It isn't helpful for growing Beloved Community.

When we become aware of our unconscious contracts, we can then act to liberate ourselves from them by releasing ourselves: "Sarah, I release you from this contract, and instead I invite you to let go of innocence as the supreme protection, to move toward humility and learning, and to embrace repairs as a way of life." Do the next exercise to explore releasing unconscious contracts for yourself.

 **EXERCISE** Releasing Unconscious Contracts
That Block Self-Compassion

I, (YOUR NAME HERE), promise myself that I will believe that:
*(Insert the compassion block connected to negative impact that resonates for you, as identified earlier in the "Discover Your Blocks to Self-Compassion" questionnaire.)*

_____

_____

_____

_____

_____

_____

Then follow the "General Worksheet to Release Unconscious Contracts" to release any of the contracts that feel true to you.

Now that we have self-compassion when we realize that we have impacted someone else negatively, what can we do to make repairs? The next skill offers us options for restoring connection.

 **NEW SKILL**
Making Repair Possible

Engaging in Authentic Dialogue is a powerful action that can lead to repair. We differentiate between dialogue and repair since we are clear that dialogue by itself often does not, and cannot, address all the harm and losses Receivers may sustain. Some losses cannot be regained. A parent who loses a child to suicide after the child endured unimaginable racist bullying will always have that loss. Dialogue makes it possible for the Receiver to share as much of their experience as possible, to make clear the breadth and depth of the loss. In dialogue the Actor can open themselves fully to the Receiver's experience, allowing themselves to be changed by what they hear. Together, through dialogue, they can mourn the irreparable harm that was sustained and the irreplaceable loss to those who survived. Together, they can arrive at a place of shared intention and commitment to enacting what is needed to mitigate as much remaining harm as can be addressed and to prevent future reoccurrences. Through dialogue, even when repair is not fully possible, together we can recommit to the vision of Beloved Community where healing and reconciliation for all is possible.

In the moment when we are reeling from impact, we can find it challenging to name that impact. We want to stay true to and express our full intensity while avoiding the moralistic judgments that are blocks to connection. From this intention we request a dialogue to support movement toward a repair. Conversely, when we learn we have impacted someone, we may find it difficult to stay fully open and curious to their experience, acknowledge impact, and begin the steps to repair. We want to navigate the moment of impact, as both Actor and Receiver, in ways that minimize further harm and create the space to ascertain what is needed to act with intention and mutual care.

What can you do when impact happens?

**Receiver:** Stop further harm. This can be as simple as saying, "Stop. That is not working for me. I need a moment."

**Actor:** When you hear a request to stop, do so. You may be confused about what is happening—still pause. Don't ask for an explanation or any engagement at the moment since the Receiver is asking for a pause for their self-regulation and self-connection; responding to you will shift their focus. Your actions that are stimulating the Receiver may be coming from your own trigger and upset; it may be difficult to tune into the Receiver's needs. If you have capacity, invite yourself into curiosity and wait. You can respond: "Okay. I'll be here when you're ready." If you do not have capacity for curiosity, use the Receiver's request for a pause as an opportunity to take action that might support self-regulation and choice for yourself.

**Receiver:** Create space for self-connection so you can decide what you need and how to proceed. After taking a deep breath to begin grounding, you could say: "I'm still off-balance here. Let me check in to see what would be supportive right now. I need (two minutes, five minutes, a break)." With practice you can do this step quickly. If you are new, ask for two or three minutes rather than a quick pause.

**Actor:** Use the pause the Receiver requested for self-empathy. Notice what is stimulated for you. This is the moment when your harsh inner critic or defensive attacker may pop up. You may experience shame, fear, judgments, and worries. You may think to yourself, *I did something wrong.* As you see the Receiver's reactions, you may interpret their emotions as a sign that disconnection is imminent. Offer yourself self-empathy for your intention as a way to attend to your needs to be seen and understood rather than ask the Receiver to acknowledge your intentions to meet those needs. You can also self-empathize with feelings coming up as you consider what you know of the impact thus far, in service of making yourself more available for the Receiver.

**Receiver:** Take time to scan yourself. Do you feel safe? Do you need to step away? If you do not feel safe, just say: "I need to take a break. I'll check in later." Then leave. See if there is someone you can turn to for accompaniment as you leave.

**Actor:** If the Receiver chooses to leave, acknowledge they are caring for themselves and let them know you're still available for connection at a later date. You may respond: "I'm open to a request to meet later if that becomes helpful. I'm curious and open to any dialogue. I'm glad you're taking a break, and I'll use the time to do my own work to support me showing up fully if we talk again." Even this may be too much for a Receiver who is stimulated. A simple "Great. I'll be here" can be enough.

As you agree to the pause, note that many of your core fears may be stimulated. Depending on your attachment style, your feelings may include curious and open (securely attached), annoyed and impatient (avoidant), alarmed aloneness and anxious (ambivalent), and tender, disconnected, or enraged (disorganized). Especially for uncomfortable feelings, it may be easier to blame the Receiver for your emotions rather than acknowledge your own needs around acceptance and belonging that were stimulated. You can use the longer break to get support. Is there a friend who can offer suggestions on what might be stimulated for the Receiver, as a way of helping you gain more understanding while the Receiver cares for themself? Can you ask for empathy or support to work on any unconscious contracts that are surfacing? Actively noticing what is emerging and choosing to meet it with warm curiosity and tenderness will interrupt any shame spirals or defensive hardening that might be forming.

**Receiver:** If you are safe, or if you have stepped away, do some silent self-empathy. Check in using this OFNR statement: "Wow, this is what just happened *(identify observation for as many layers as you have access to)*. I feel *(identify feelings)* because I'm needing *(identify needs)*." Breathe in again.

**Actor:** Continue with self-empathy, empathy from another, or self-education as needed.

**Receiver:** Once you're connected to your needs in the moment, check in further with yourself. Are you wanting to have a dialogue around repair now, or do you need more time for deeper self-empathy or empathy from another?

If you need more time: You can notice: "Wow. I'm still reeling. That was big and I'm not clear what I'm needing right now. I'm glad for the pause so that I could get a breath, but I don't want to try to talk about what's come up for me yet. I'm going to take some more time and get support to understand what I need." You can then ask the Actor: "Are you open to me checking back in with you once I have a better sense of how I'd like to proceed?"

If you're ready to jump in: Ask for a Dialogue to Be Heard. Going through this dialogue can be the first step of the repair. At its conclusion you will have more clarity if you next need a Dialogue for Healing, a Dialogue for Shared Understanding, or a Dialogue for Solution. When you ask for a dialogue, it's helpful to let the person know if you want them to hold a lot of intensity, and/or if you're open to hearing their experience. There is no right way to be. Here are some sample statements:

- "I'm pretty devastated right now. I want to share what's coming up for me and I know I've got some charge. I'm willing to try being real and share it, but I need trust you're willing to try to hear me fully. Is there something that will support you if you feel overwhelmed?"
- "I'm really angry right now. I'm willing to say why, but at this moment, I'm not ready to listen to your experience. If you think you can hear what's up for me, and get support elsewhere, I'm willing to share."
- "I'm really confused about what happened, and I'm not really clear on what I want to say yet. If you can listen to me and reflect back what is important to me, it will help. I'd like you to commit to reflecting just what you hear me say because I'll get overwhelmed trying to sort through my stuff and your stuff. Do you have the capacity to listen without explaining while I try to get clear on what I need?"

**Actor:** If the Receiver asks for more time, say yes. Remember, the intensity/depth of their reaction likely includes needs related to internal and systemic level stimuli, in addition to whatever external stimuli you provided. Their reaction is not just about you. More space for their self-connection will benefit you both in attending to all that is true, not just the slice they can most easily access without reflection.

For any other request of the Receiver, check in on what you need for yourself to show up in the way the Receiver is requesting. For instance, you might benefit from more empathy from a friend before entering the dialogue or from having a support person or facilitator present during the dialogue to keep you on track with how you want to show up. Aim to support the Receiver in what they need to engage in dialogue without dropping your own needs.

IN CLOSING

## Growing Our Capacity for Authentic Dialogue

In this chapter we brought our attachment patterns into our consideration of racism. We also introduced the structure of Authentic Dialogue and reviewed ways it can be used to navigate the moment of negative impact and move toward repair in questions related to racism. Both of these actions strengthen our secure attachment and make us more resilient, and this in turn grows our capacity to create Beloved Community.

In Chapter 8 we learn about microaggressions—what they are, how they do harm, and how to let self-compassion help us receive less harm from microaggressions and do less harm through them.

# 8

# Microaggressions and Catching Impact

ANTIRACISM CONCEPT
**Microaggressions**

This chapter concerns the way that we unconsciously reinforce racial and cultural stereotypes through our actions, conveying the stay-in-your-place messages that are called "microaggressions." They are so unconscious and deeply rooted that if we don't know what they are, we can't stop using them and continually do harm without knowing it. Let's first look at the definition of racial microaggressions. Dr. Chester Pierce, an African American psychiatrist, is credited with introducing the term in the 1970s. D. W. Sue and colleagues offer this seminal definition: "Racial microaggressions are brief and commonplace daily verbal, behavioral, or environmental indignities, whether intentional or unintentional, that communicate hostile, derogatory, or negative racial slights and insults toward people of color."[36]

The prefix "micro" in the word "microaggression" refers not to the intensity or magnitude of the experience, but instead to the interpersonal nature of these interactions that occur between people across groups. They can be contrasted with macroaggressions, which refer to policies and systems that have adverse impacts at the group level. The term has been expanded to include impacts experienced by members of social groups that experience lower rank (e.g., folks with disabilities, women, folks who identify as LGBTQIA2S+, religious minorities, etc.).

Isabel Wilkerson's scholarship illuminated another purpose of microaggressions.[37] They (un)consciously serve to reinforce the subordinate social position of groups in society. Wilkerson describes US society as embodying a caste system since its founding, with Black people relegated to the lowest caste, white people to the highest caste, and people from other ethnic groups generally distributed in the middle castes. Your race defined—often legally but many times through social norms and expectations—where you could live, who you could love, what kind of work you did, and so much more. We use microaggressions to reinforce social norms and return people who defy the (un)conscious expectations we have for a person of their caste to their place. Microaggressions convey coded messages that remind the "transgressing" person that members of their caste are not supposed to be highly educated, wealthy, or live or shop in certain communities, for instance. The activation of caste norms stimulates microaggressions that either express surprise that the person is departing from caste norms, marks them as an exception ("You're not my nurse? You're the doctor?!"), or attempts to return them to caste appropriate behavior ("You've got the wrong door. The entrance to the balcony section is over there.").

An important element of microaggressions is the pervasiveness of the experience. Global Majority folks experience microaggressions ALL THE TIME! Roxy describes: When I go to the store, I am offered price checks and directed to lower-priced items. When I interact with medical professionals, they often use simple language that leaves out nuanced medical information. When I go to teach, people ask me where the teacher is, compliment me on how well I speak, and express delighted amazement about my academic credentials. All these are examples of the myriad racial microaggressions I experience in daily life.

White people often take offense at having their whiteness referred to. Here is the reason that referring to someone's whiteness is not a microaggression. Microaggressions carry an implicit message about a group's lower rank in society. If someone tells me their identity, referring to that identity by calling them male, female, trans, Black, white, Asian, Latine, Indigenous is the same as identifying that they are tall or short, brown-eyed or blue-eyed, long-haired or short-haired. Descriptive words are not inherently negative or positive. It's when those words become proxies for hidden meanings and stereotypes about a group with lower social rank that they become problematic. When we talk about needing "extra support for Black students," when we really mean "students who are not academically successful," we are conveying a hidden message. That message is rooted in stereotypes that Black students are not academically successful and conveys a message that any Black student at that site will need academic support. It reinforces caste stereotypes about the intelligence and potential for achievement of Black people. That message is quite different from "we need extra support for students who are struggling academically."

Many people in the United States don't know how to talk about race. We don't yet have a model for talking about and responding to exactly the kinds of situations that microaggressions describe—differential treatment of members of one group that stem from (un)consciously held beliefs about members of that group. Without a more nuanced framing or a model that can encompass the complexity of a socially constructed phenomenon that has been used to impact people, with horrific real-world consequences, we're stuck. How do we hold the truth that we don't believe race is real and don't want to act on such painful stories about people, and yet still do so because we've internalized the racist patterns of behavior that are so much a part of our culture?

Someone in that stuck place might, when called in after committing a microaggression, resort to a limited, flawed strategy. We might, consciously or unconsciously, believe that the only way to avoid the painful self-judgments that might arise if we admit we have committed a microaggression or a racist act is to make any mention of race bad. We demonize any discussion centered on race and assume that it is the mention of race that is the root of the problem. Doing so requires us to ignore the stereotypes, the painful impact, the historical inequities affecting the person who has been harmed and say, "It's all equivalently problematic." This is a rhetorical move that shuts down the conversation, silences the receiver of a microaggression, and allows a white person to see their pain about race as equal to the pain about race a Global Majority person holds. It's not a move that leads to any hope for the kind of authentic, albeit painful, dialogue that is needed to help us move from the unconscious exercise of stereotypes and caste norms into a truly more equitable world.

 **WORKSHEET**
## The Coded Messages in Microaggressions

Here are a few of the many examples of microaggression themes identified by Sue and his colleagues.[38] Can you identify the coded message(s) in the microaggression?

EXAMPLE:

**Theme:** Alien in one's own land.

**Microaggressions:** "Where are you from?" "Go back to your country!" "Learn to speak English."

**Message:** People who look like you are not really from the United States. You don't belong here.

**Theme:** Color blindness.

**Microaggressions:** "We're all the same." "I don't see color." "We're all human."

**Message:** _____

_____

_____

_____

**Theme:** Ascription of intellectual inferiority.

**Microaggressions:** "Which Harvard did you get into?" "Did you get a sports scholarship?" "Do you need help reading that?" "You scored really high for a Black person!"

**Message:** _____

_____

_____

_____

**Theme:** Ascription of intelligence.

**Microaggressions:** To an Asian person I just met: "Can you help me with the statistics homework?" "I bet you don't even have to study." "Are you a pre-med major?"

**Message:** _____

_____

_____

_____

**Theme:** Assumption of criminality.

**Microaggressions:** "Do you have any pot?" Following a Global Majority person while they shop. Locking your car door when a Black/Latine man walks by.

**Message:** _____

_____

_____

_____

**Theme:** Pathologizing cultural values/communication styles.

**Microaggressions:** Encouraging Asian/Latine students who don't raise their hands to speak. "You're being too loud." "Don't be so submissive. Stand up for yourself."

**Message:** _____

_____

_____

_____

**Theme:** Assumed universality of Global Majority experience within group.

**Microaggressions:** Asking the Black student in class to speak on behalf of all Black people. "If you identify as Latine, you must speak Spanish."

**Message:** _____

_____

_____

_____

COMMON BLOCKS
## Conflating the Systemic and the Individual

One issue that people experience when having conversations about racism is the tendency to confuse where the source of their challenge lies. This occurs in several ways. People who try to speak about racism are often accused of being "difficult" or making their peers uncomfortable. The individual person is being judged as the problem when the true problem is racism and the racial inequities they are trying to address. This leads to the exclusion of the person rather than attempts to change the system.

The converse happens when people are unable to bear conversations about systemic racism. They assume that a person who raises a systemic issue in response to their behavior is actually calling them racist. This stance ignores the reality that systemic racism does exist and can benefit a person who is white or white-adjacent (Global Majority people who are granted some of the privileges associated with whiteness because they are not Black, Latine, or Indigenous, or have lighter skin) whether or not that person actively seeks out that benefit. By insisting on a focus on the individual—"I didn't make that law, I wasn't alive then, I don't benefit from that"—they shift focus away from the systemic.

WORKSHEET
## Analyzing Who Is Served

Recall a time when a challenge related to systemic racism arose between individuals. Reflect on how it was to address this challenge.

Did you notice either individual use the strategy of shifting the focus from the systemic to focus on individual responsibility?

_____

_____

Who made these shifts?

_____

_____

Who benefited from the shift—what needs were met for them?

_____

_____

Who did not benefit from the shift—what needs were not met for them?

_____

_____

Reflect on how these shifts supported or hindered the exploration of the issue.

_____

_____

NEUROSCIENCE CONCEPT
## Implicit Biases and the Default Mode Network

Every form of racism, including microaggressions, does observable, measurable harm to the brain and the health of the person receiving the racism. The more a person experiences racial discrimination, the more automatically vigilant their brain becomes, disrupting the stress network and making it more reactive.[39] The more microaggressions a person receives, the worse their immune system response and their heart health.[40] So every time there is a slip into verbally reinforcing someone's lower-caste status ("You're so well-spoken!"), the lower-caste person is being hurt. Caste and racism are invisible in all the areas where a person has privilege and status, so it is impossible to just learn this once and be done. It is necessary to practice, practice, practice, and learn and receive feedback, or people with more privilege and status will just be walking around doing continual unconscious harm.

Without even knowing it, we are all effortlessly sorting people into different racial groups based on how they look, and we continually implicitly generate racial bias, which affects how we think and act, no matter what racial group we belong to. Our unconscious racial differentiation makes our brains create two categories: our own race and other races. Our brains prioritize our own race, letting us have empathy and imagination about people of our own race, lighting up brain areas like the medial prefrontal cortex and the inferior frontal gyrus.[41] These areas coordinate with autobiographical memories and social knowledge. But the other-race brain areas—the fusiform gyrus, the inferior parietal lobule, and the amygdala—connect us with watchfulness and alarm.[42] The more we know this about our brain, the more we can ground ourselves in humility and awareness, receive feedback, make repairs, and grow new intentions as we go.

JOURNALING PROMPT
**Taking Responsibility for Our Brains**

Choose a different racial or cultural group than your own, one that has less power than yours.

Make a list of the way your own group views this different group.

_____

_____

_____

_____

Review the types of microaggressions shown in "The Coded Messages in Microaggressions" worksheet, and choose one you are likely to slip into, or know that you have slipped into.

_____

_____

_____

_____

_____

Write a sample dialogue that contains the microaggression.

_____

_____

_____

_____

Rewrite the conversation without the microaggression, choosing a different path, and imagine what kind of dialogue and quality of connection could result.

_____

_____

_____

_____

_____

_____

COMMON BLOCKS **to Self-Compassion for Receivers of Microaggressions**

The most important elements for self-compassion when receiving microaggressions are naming, accompaniment, and releasing any belief that the microaggressions are true. These things, added together, help the immune system and create resilience. We name the truth of what is happening and acknowledge that microaggressions are actual acts of harm; we either accompany ourselves or get accompaniment from others in seeing the big systemic picture and releasing any beliefs that the microaggressions are true; and we either offer ourselves understanding or get some support from others to name our very real emotional response. For example, we might feel anger or contempt or exhaustion or sorrow or alarmed aloneness.

When we make sure that we get to tell the truth and are resonated with in such situations, we allow full self-compassion and compassion to flow. But sometimes we have made agreements with ourselves to be tough, or impervious, or to handle everything on our own. These agreements block self-compassion. The "What Are My Self-Compassion Blocks?" questionnaire will help you find out if you have any agreements with yourself that block self-compassion.

 QUESTIONNAIRE **(for Those Who Receive Microaggressions)**
**What Are My Self-Compassion Blocks?**

*Give the following statements points from 0–10*
*(0 = not true, 10 = very true):*

\_\_\_\_ I need to handle things on my own.
\_\_\_\_ No one will ever know when I am hurt.
\_\_\_\_ My feelings are a burden for others.
\_\_\_\_ I am numb.
\_\_\_\_ No one can touch me.

\_\_\_\_ Discriminatory statements can't hurt me.

\_\_\_\_ I will be better at everything (or some things) than anyone else.

\_\_\_\_ I'm too sensitive.

\_\_\_\_ This shouldn't hurt me.

\_\_\_\_ I dissociate when people make microaggressions.

\_\_\_\_ **TOTAL**

**SCORING:**

**60-100:** You have significant blocks to self-compassion. You have difficulty allowing yourself to acknowledge that you have been the Receiver of microaggressions or that they have an adverse impact. You do not give yourself permission to need support and judge yourself harshly for needing it.

**30-59:** You find self-compassion is a challenge. You struggle with accepting that you are impacted by microaggressions. Although it may feel incredibly vulnerable to do so because of your self-judgments, you can reach out at times for empathic support from others to bolster your self-compassion capacity.

**0-29:** You are able to access self-compassion. You recognize that microaggressions are a challenge for anyone. You might notice initial messages that say you should deal with them on your own, but you are able to overcome those messages and, leaning into interdependence, reach out for support when needed.

 COMMON BLOCKS **to Self-Compassion for Those with Privilege**

It is very difficult for us to learn about microaggressions if we judge ourselves for not being perfect, or for being socially awkward, or for not knowing everything before it happens. Since we can all have microaggressions come out of our mouths any time we are the privilege holders, and the only real remedies for microaggressions are humility and the willingness to learn and receive feedback, these self-judgments only get in the way. The "What Are My Perfectionism-Related Blocks?" questionnaire will help you discover any agreements you might have with yourself that block self-compassion.

QUESTIONNAIRE (for Those with Privilege)
## What Are My Perfectionism-Related Blocks?

*Give the following statements points from 0–10*
*(0 = not true, 10 = very true):*

\_\_\_\_ I am always careful to do things right.

\_\_\_\_ I will never let anyone make me wrong.

\_\_\_\_ I will believe that it is dangerous to be wrong.

\_\_\_\_ I should never make mistakes.

\_\_\_\_ I don't forgive myself for my errors and mistakes.

\_\_\_\_ I remember my faux pas for years.

\_\_\_\_ I should be perfectly socially graceful.

\_\_\_\_ I should be perfect.

\_\_\_\_ I will reject myself completely when I make mistakes.

\_\_\_\_ My worthiness depends on my perfection.

\_\_\_\_ **TOTAL**

**SCORING:**

**80–100:** You score very high on perfectionism, and it may be hindering you in your commitment to Beloved Community. You may hold others to the same high standards that you apply to yourself. Everyone, even you, belongs to Beloved Community. You might enjoy releasing three or more of these contracts, the ones you scored most highly.

**60–79:** You probably are most demanding of yourself, with more grace given to others. Release any contracts you scored with an 8 or higher, and check back in to see how your self-compassion is doing about your brain leading you astray.

**40–59:** You are sometimes anxious about doing things right, and sometimes you feel more at ease in the world. Track your anxiety to see whether it has any correlation with ways that you demand perfectionism of yourself, and release any contracts that are involved.

**20–39:** Congratulations for either your natural secure attachment, or for all the work you have done to create self-compassion. You are in a fairly balanced place in relation to perfectionism.

**0–19:** Look for unconscious contracts that keep you from fully engaging in or participating in the world. You will know yourself whether you have done an extraordinary amount of work, or if there is some way that you are holding yourself back from full engagement with life.

Next is an exercise to walk you through releasing the unconscious contracts that concern you.

 EXERCISE **Releasing Unconscious Contracts**
**(That Block Self-Compassion in Relationship to Microaggressions)**

I, (YOUR NAME HERE), promise myself that I will:
*(Insert the compassion block connected to microaggressions that resonates for you.)*

_____

_____

_____

Then follow the "General Worksheet to Release Unconscious Contracts" to release any of the contracts that feel true to you.

Again, the invitation to self-compassion opens the doorway to a clearer ability to see, which allows us to learn the next new skill: seeing systemically.

**NEW SKILL Deepening Our Ability to Identify Systemic Observations**

At their root racial microaggressions are grounded in patterns of oppression that privilege whiteness at the expense of all other groups. When we experience or witness a microaggression, we might struggle to know how to talk about it in a way that demonstrates where the impact is coming from. Increasing our capacity to link the microaggression to the oppressive systems and white supremacy culture that gave birth to them can increase our efficacy. When we name not just the external observation (the action or words that were taken that we identified as a microaggression) but the systemic observation that gave birth to the microaggression and the coded message we received, we establish shared understanding about the depth of the stimulus that impacted us.

**WORKSHEET Connecting Microaggressions and Systemic Observations**

Here are some examples of microaggressions that Roxy or her family have experienced. Read the microaggression and try to identify both the systemic observations that it is grounded in and the coded messages it sends.

EXAMPLE:

**External Observation:** Roxy chats with her white friend and her friend's mother while waiting to be seated at a restaurant. The hostess who comes to seat the party stands with her back to Roxy, and smiling at the two white women, she asks: "So, that will be a party of two?"

**Systemic Observation:** For a significant portion of the United States's existence, Black people were prohibited from eating and participating in certain commercial spaces.

**Coded Messages:** White people and Black people are not equal and cannot be friends. White people are more valuable customers than Black people and deserve priority service.

**External Observation:** When the line for first class is called and Roxy joins it, the gate agent tells Roxy they're only seating first class now and asks Roxy to wait for her section to be called.

**Systemic Observation:** _____

_____

_____

_____

_____

**Coded Messages:** _____

_____

_____

_____

**External Observation:** While Roxy is out with her toddler, a stranger says: "She's so pretty. She doesn't look Black at all."

**Systemic Observation:** _____

_____

_____

_____

_____

**Coded Messages:** _____

_____

_____

_____

_____

**External Observation:** While visiting a prospective college, a staff person asks Roxy's teen: "Are you going to play basketball for us?"

**Systemic Observation:** _____

_____

_____

_____

_____

**Coded Messages:** _____

_____

_____

_____

_____

**External Observation:** Someone Roxy doesn't know touches her hair while saying: "Wow, it feels so spongy!"

**Systemic Observation:** _____

_____

_____

_____

_____

**Coded Messages:** _____

_____

_____

_____

_____

**External Observation:** Someone tells Roxy's child: "You have good hair—it's only a little bit nappy."

**Systemic Observation:** _____

_____

_____

_____

_____

**Coded Messages:** _____

_____

_____

_____

_____

**External Observation:** A white man says to Roxy: "I don't see you as Black. We all bleed red."

**Systemic Observation:** _____

_____

_____

_____

_____

**Coded Messages:** _____

_____

_____

_____

_____

**External Observation:** Roxy's son's coach decides to talk to the team about the Black Lives Matter movement and asks her son to share about it with the team.

**Systemic Observation:** _____

_____

_____

_____

**Coded Messages:** _____

_____

_____

_____

_____

**External Observation:** *(Write your own external observation describing a microaggression you received or committed.)*

_____

_____

_____

_____

_____

**Systemic Observation:** _____

_____

_____

_____

**Coded Messages:** _____

_____

_____

_____

IN CLOSING

## Warm Curiosity

Surprisingly, even though what we're trying to see and change is the large-scale, systemic ways that racism traces a path through our lives, one of the most effective ways to overcome our unconscious, implicit bias is very personal: it is to look at people we might consider to be outside of our group and to wonder, for example, what their favorite games were when they were ten-year-olds. This simple act of warm curiosity about something personal that can be so global and so shared takes the other person out of the "other" category and makes them "us."

Until we have truly built Beloved Community, we still need to be vigilant for the ways that microaggressions can impact our interactions, even with our closest friends and families. However, the more we all make each other "us," the healthier everyone's brains will have the opportunity to be and the more we can recognize our shared humanity. In Chapter 9 we address the ways that we can collapse and be silent, rather than taking action and expressing ourselves.

# 9

# Collapse, Silence, and Choice

ANTIRACISM CONCEPT
## Silence and Collapse

Silence in the face of racism—whether from the Receiver, the Bystander, or the Actor—is a reaction that stems from many different sources. Since there can be many meanings to silence, we want to understand what our silence might mean to others and return a degree of choice, as much as is possible, to our use of silence.

Nervous system collapse is one often unconscious reaction to racism that can result in silence. When we collapse, the nervous system slows and we have difficulty engaging in action, including speaking up. Our silence in this moment reflects our vastly reduced capacity for action. We may be horrified by what we are experiencing or witnessing, and would choose, had we access to our full capacity, to act. We stay silent because we simply do not have the capacity to respond with the same expediency and efficacy as we normally would. If you have collapsed or experienced immobilization in response to racism, review the upcoming section on immobilization. You might also consider requesting a friend or colleague to join you and offer support when you enter dialogue.

We may consciously choose silence as well. Receivers and Bystanders may choose silence as a way of asserting choice. Global

Majority people experience so many acts of racism that we do not have the capacity to respond to each one. We may choose silence and take no action in response to a specific act of racism in order to conserve energy and choose where we wish to place our resources. We may be exhausted from our efforts to intervene and support change in a system and are silent out of self-care. Silence does not mean we condone what we are experiencing, although an Actor may assume that it does: "See, you're not bothered—you know I'm just joking, right honey?"

It's important to recognize there can be a gap between the needs we intend to meet by our silence, and the meaning others take from it. One way this shows up is with Bystander silence. A Bystander may be silent out of collapse, freeze, or even their best guess of what the Receiver might want. A Bystander may be exhausted because they've spoken up so often to advocate for change, and the Actor's behavior does not change. A Receiver or others who are not familiar with the Bystander's past attempts at advocacy may not know how to interpret the current silence. They may leave the situation thinking, "Wow, no one said a single thing. They must all share the same beliefs," and decide not to return.

Transparency about the reason for silence, when possible, can help to reduce the disconnections that might occur. We might not want to put energy into speaking up yet again, but there are a range of responses that we might consider. We could share our limits: "If we stay on this topic, I'll head out now." It could be: "Not okay. Just stop." Even the simple "Ouch" is a way to let impact be known without engaging more than we wish. We could also be strategic in when and with whom we speak. If my concern is about having to educate white people about why something is racist, I might choose to speak at a later time only to the Global Majority people who were present or others with whom I already have shared understanding.

ANTIRACISM CONCEPT
## Negative versus Positive Peace

We recognize that sometimes our silence can be a strategy for seeking peace and harmony. If we don't speak up, there is no conflict. Yet it is important to differentiate between positive peace and negative peace. Negative peace exists in the absence of action to address harm. In spaces defined by negative peace, attempts to bring attention to systemic inequities and acts of racism, and the resulting tension and pain, are judged as violent by the Actor and some Bystanders.

Beloved Community is built on positive peace that rests on our action for justice and to end harm, not on our silence. Positive peace can only exist through our active care and commitment to attend to the needs of all human beings. Positive peace, in direct opposition to negative peace, requires us to draw attention to harm and take steps to address it. It depends on us to speak up, to interrupt, to name, and to address harm when we encounter it. Positive peace requires our active advocacy and engagement in dialogue and welcomes the tension and pain that are a part of growth and change.

JOURNALING PROMPT
## The Meaning of Silence

Think of a moment when you were silent in the presence of racism. Describe what happened. Journal about your silence. How choiceful did it feel? Was silence the response you would have chosen no matter what, or was it the only option that felt available to you? Perhaps it wasn't even a choice? Did you collapse or freeze? If you are aware of others making meaning of your silence, write out that meaning. Journal about the needs your silence met and did not meet for you, the Receiver, the Bystander, and the Actor. As you consider all the needs you identify, write about how you see your actions contributing to positive peace or negative peace.

_____

_____

_____

_____

_____

_____

### NEUROSCIENCE CONCEPT
## The Nervous System in Immobilization

One way that the nervous system responds to messages of safety and danger is that we become activated, with higher heart rate and blood pressure and reduced ability to accurately read others with empathy. There is another option too: we can become immobilized when we are shocked and helpless. Sometimes this means we can't move because we are so tense, and sometimes this means we can't move because we've lost all our energy. We can experience shock when we are the target of systemic racism. We can also be shocked when we receive feedback that we are inflicting systemic racism on others with negative impact, including unconscious exclusion or microaggressions, which we now know do actual physical, immune-system, and mental health harm to the people we are impacting.

Leftover messages of danger from childhood can tell us that we are helpless or powerless even when we are not. When we believe that we have no power, our heart rate decreases, our blood pressure falls, our digestion stops, our immune system stops working, and our faces and muscles lose their tone.[43] Becoming immobilized is completely natural and was very important when we were children. However, it is less likely to serve us as adults with agency and power—the power to stand up for ourselves or others, whether as Receivers or Bystanders; the power to point out that racism is being enacted; the power to choose not to respond when it would be dangerous; the power to listen and understand the impact of our actions; and the power to make repairs when we have perpetuated systemic racism.

We tend to lose energy and the ability to move, or to freeze with tension, when we are valuing needs for safety or harmony over our own needs for expression. This could mean needs for keeping our job, not being thrown off public transit or out of a public place, or prioritizing someone else's need for safety or harmony. We also tend to become immobilized when we are locked in shame, perhaps because people told us that we were bad when we were children, or because we have been punished or lost relationships because we made mistakes. Immobilization can be a very common response to all three positions in systemic racism: the Receiver, the Bystander, and the Actor.

**JOURNALING PROMPT**
## When Do You Freeze?

Choose which position in systemic racism you would like to work with: Receiver, Bystander, or Actor

My position: _____

Describe a moment of immobilization in your experience of systemic racism:

_____

_____

_____

_____

Now imagine turning toward yourself in that moment and freezing everyone who is present except yourself.

The best remedy for immobilization is warm self-gentleness. Instead of judging ourselves, we have a new option—self-compassion. We can use our own names when we speak to ourselves with understanding and care, for example:

Roxy, Sarah, no wonder you have frozen. Would you like some acknowledgment of what is at stake? Are you not responding in real time to this precarious situation for fear of danger and generating more damage? Do you need more time to practice your new skills? Do you need more time to be able to find and release the unconscious contracts that have you convinced that no one wants to hear your voice? Do you want to speak up even when you don't remember your skills? Do you need to be held with gentleness, dignity, and respect, even if you are never able to speak out the way you wish you could? Do you long for your voice to flow freely and with self-confident rootedness in what matters most to you, always holding to the values of Beloved Community?

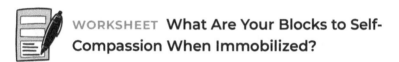 **WORKSHEET** **What Are Your Blocks to Self-Compassion When Immobilized?**

In this Time Travel to your moment of immobilization, is it possible for your current self to have warmth and compassion for your past self? Does your past self permit you to look at yourself with warmth and compassion?

☐ Yes          ☐ No

If there are self-judgments, what are they?

_____

_____

_____

Look for blame of self or blame of others. Both kinds of blame will stop you from practicing new skills. What happens if you just start a sentence with the words "I blame…"?

I blame… _____

_____

_____

Review the "Needs and Values" chart in the Appendix (Figure 6). What are the qualities you would most like to embody in this moment? Choose your top three.

_____

_____

_____

Ask your past self, "Do you wish for… (*and name these three needs*)." Take a moment to breathe these needs in. What would it be like to experience the living gifts of these needs and to savor them, in addition to simply naming them? This process helps the needs to be more accessible to our bodies and our imaginations.

Are these three needs self-protective? (For example, do you long for protection, safety, or privacy? Or for someone else to take action?)

☐ Yes     ☐ No

If the needs you chose are self-protective, return to the "Needs and Values" chart in the Appendix and choose three needs for everyone involved in the situation.

_____

_____

_____

Ask your past self, "Do you wish for... (*and name these three needs*)." Take a moment to breathe these needs in. What would it be like to experience the living gifts of these needs and to savor them, in addition to simply naming them?

How does your past self respond?

_____

_____

_____

If there is a lot of shame, self-blame, or blame of others still present in the memory, you are probably trying to live out an undoable and unconscious contract.

If I have an undoable contract here, it might be:

_____

_____

_____

Does your past self relax at all? If there has been any relaxation, invite your past self to join you in present time. What is it like to have your past self with you?

_____

_____

_____

If your past self does not relax at all, bookmark this memory and check in with it again at the end of this handbook. There may be more contracts to release or skills you may learn through the rest of the handbook that will support your past self.

NEW SKILL
## Connection Requests

When harm has happened, especially in the context of a relationship that matters to us, we typically want to focus on clearly and completely conveying information about the harm—that is, the *content* of what happened. At times, we may do so in ways that actually damage the connection between speaker and listener rather than make it stronger. A speaker may insist on sharing information at a time when the listener is physically exhausted and struggles to receive it. Although the listener eventually succeeds in showing understanding of the speaker's content, they also leave with resentment and a firm belief that their needs are not important to the speaker. Conversely, a listener may be so intent on deepening their understanding of the speaker's experience that they keep asking question after question, not noticing the speaker's increasing distress until the speaker walks away, distraught. We want to hold the *process* of dialogue with the same attention and care as we hold the content.

Using connection requests allows us to ask for what we need to attend to the quality of our connection. Connection requests are thus an important part of the Authentic Dialogue process. With connection requests we can fine-tune how we are with each other so that even the act of being in dialogue can be restorative, independent of any outcome. Miki Kashtan and Inbal Kashtan describe several types of connection requests that one can make.[44] Let's go through each type of connection request and discuss how we might use them in Authentic Dialogue:

1. **Willingness for dialogue.** We begin Authentic Dialogues by checking for consent. If I want to be heard, I might ask someone if they are willing to listen to me. I might be more specific about the type of listening I want. I might ask: "Are you willing to listen and only reflect back the feelings and needs you hear me say?"

Someone else might say: "I'd love you to listen and let me speak uninterrupted for the first ten minutes." Conversely, if I want to understand someone's experience, I might ask if now is a good time for them to share what they were distressed about the last time we met.

2. **Reflection of content.** Once the dialogue is under way, we want to know that "message sent was message received." Regular checks in which we ask the listener to share what they heard can confirm for us that the essence of what we are sharing was received. The listener can also initiate checks to be sure they are understanding the speaker accurately, but does so while being mindful that the checks for understanding are supporting the *speaker's* need to be understood and not the *listener's* need for understanding if that would be at cost to the speaker. The more tense the situation, or the more emotional intensity is present, the more frequent the checks either might make. These checks are important especially when the content of discussion, the memory of a harm that happened, is triggering for the speaker. If the listener is consistently reflecting and checking for understanding, the speaker will experience these reflections themselves as an expression of tangible, in-the-moment care—a perhaps small but meaningful and hopeful antidote to the previous harm.

3. **Empathic reflection.** We can ask the listener to share what they understand is important to us as they hear us speak. This type of reflection request can help a listener unfamiliar with Nonviolent Communication understand what to focus on when listening empathically. If the listener is familiar with empathy, we can simply ask for an empathic reflection or a feelings and needs guess. As a listener, if we notice judgments rising in us as we listen to the speaker, intentionally shifting our focus to hear them empathically can open our hearts to them. As a speaker, hearing

someone reflect back our feelings and needs can relieve our
worries about being judged.

4. **Understanding our impact.** When we share our truth, we may
have curiosity about the listener's experience of hearing us. If so,
we can ask the listener about their experience. We might simply
ask: "Can you tell me what comes up in you when you hear me
name this?" If we are sharing traumatic content, we might worry
that they are struggling to ground themselves. We can check on
their emotional regulation: "I know what I shared was pretty
intense. Do you need some space before we continue?" If we
share the intensity of the impact they had on us, we may worry
they are feeling disconnected from us or judging themselves.
We then might check: "I'm curious if you're experiencing any
judgments hearing what it was like for me?" We can choose to
shift our focus to the process and check on the effect of our words,
both out of care for the listener and to increase the likelihood
of us being heard as we would wish. When we learn that the
listener has been deeply impacted by our words, our response to
them can signal that we are holding their needs along with our
own. If we realize that the listener is struggling with the impact,
we might choose to pause our expression. We can do so out of
care, to create space for them to self-connect or receive empathy
from another. We may also do so out of self-care if we prefer to
speak when the listener is more resourced to stay with our full
authenticity.

5. **Advancing solutions.** This final type of connection request
supports our capacity to take action. With this type of connection
request, the focus is not on the specific strategy we adopt—the
content of the request—but on the quality of our connection
and our trust in how we are holding each other's needs. We
may first check the other's willingness to move toward strategy.
We might ask: "Do you think we have enough understanding

of what's important to each other that we can start thinking of some strategies that could work for both of us?" As we generate strategies, we can make requests that assess the extent to which a strategy under consideration can meet needs. For example: "I'm worried that we haven't found a way to attend to all four needs we identified as most crucial, but you may feel some urgency to reach a decision as we near the end of our scheduled time. Are you truly hopeful this strategy is sufficient, or would you prefer to see if it is possible to extend our meeting time or find a new time to meet so we can continue exploring strategies?" Even after we agree upon a strategy, we can check around barriers to implementing the strategy. "Is there anything I don't understand about your current workload that would prevent you from following through with the outreach as planned?"

When we make connection requests, our hope is to support sufficient ease and flow in the dialogue that we each leave with a sense of our mutual mattering. Connection requests are most powerful and are easiest to receive when we understand why the person is making the request. If as speaker we ask "Can you tell me what you heard?" the listener may be upset: "You don't think I was paying attention?" If we are transparent about our experience and the needs we're trying to meet, the listener may be more receptive. We might say instead: "When I'm nervous, I often don't track the things that I wanted to share. Can you tell me what you heard so I can double check if there's more I wanted to share?" A different request for a different example: "I realize I'm so used to sharing what that teacher said to me, I forget that it's a shock when people hear it for the first time. I'd like to check how you are after hearing this so that we can decide if a break now would help you regroup and return to strategizing."

WORKSHEET
## Connection Requests

Use this scenario to come up with each of the five types of connection requests.

> You are a white volunteer at a local Black-led organization that is protesting a series of regulations contributing to gentrification. The group held a recent press event for some of the organization's leaders. The team from the organization consisted of five of the Black founders. You and another white volunteer were there in a supportive role. At the event reporters attempted to speak to you and the other white person, ignoring the Black leadership. You stepped back and sat down at the sidelines. As you watched, the other white volunteer answered several of the reporter's questions before redirecting them to the Black leaders. A few days later, you see the white volunteer. You're angry at them.

What is a request you can make to assess "willingness to dialogue"?

_____

_____

_____

> The volunteer agrees to talk. You're still quite angry. From a place of trigger, you say: "I'm so tired of people like you who don't know when to step back. You didn't make space for the elders to talk about their problems and then hogged the spotlight. I feel sick seeing you on TV when the founders barely got the same amount of time."

What is a request for content reflection that you can make?

_____

_____

_____

What is a request for an empathic reflection that you can make?

_____

_____

_____

What is a request you can make to understand the impact of how you spoke?

_____

_____

_____

As you play out this scenario, imagine you have worked through the process involved and you have a sense you both understand the importance of moving back and centering the voices of those whom you choose to support.

What is a request you can make to move the discussion to focusing on possible action steps?

_____

_____

_____

### IN CLOSING
## Being Gentle with Ourselves

The wonderful thing about working with this material is that we become more self-compassionate in moments where we don't know what to do. We also begin to develop more skills and options for things to do or say when harm is being done. In those moments when we are too overwhelmed or too much is at stake to make expression possible, we have learned to be very gentle and welcoming with ourselves. We are also developing Authentic Dialogue skills to provide new possibilities when we are Receivers, Bystanders, and even when we notice that we are Actors in white supremacy culture. We are much more equipped to move forward into co-creating Beloved Community, wherever we go.

Chapter 10 explores possible obstacles to effective antiracist efforts, such as reactivity, urgency, defensiveness, and denial as strategies for survival—why we react in these ways, and how to address them.

# 10

# "...Is Paved with Good Intentions"

ANTIRACISM CONCEPT
**Reactivity and Urgency**

As we saw earlier, our anger is a powerful compass pointing to our care. When we understand the deep passion we have for change, we may experience both reactivity and a sense of urgency. Reactivity—becoming stimulated or responding with intensity larger than one might expect for a given stimulus—is a fairly common reaction when we understand the extent of the issue before us and the degree of harm it represents. We might respond with a fierce anger to new examples of inequity or to events that simply remind us of it. Our anger is another reminder of the intensity of our longing for change. We might respond with disdain and yet more anger toward someone we see making choices that uphold or fail to address the issues we care about—it's a sign of our longing for solidarity and shared commitment for change.

While our reactivity is understandable, if it goes unchecked, it can contribute to disconnection from the very people with whom a natural alignment seemed possible. So many groups—Global Majority, white, and mixed—fall apart from within. The threads of shared purpose and commitment to change are not enough to hold the group together when reactivity is there. To be clear, there are many complex reasons why groups fall apart. Even without the impact of reactivity, the work of building organizations, joining those with shared purpose working in solidarity, is complex and requires attention to numerous elements.

Just as we want to find ways to work with our own reactivity, we also want to examine our response to other people's reactivity. If we are only able to stay in relationship with someone if they show up in ways that prioritize our comfort, we are not doing the hard work required to build Beloved Community. Reflecting on this dynamic is especially important for those who hold privilege and are in relationship with more impacted folks. Some people can only be an "ally" with Global Majority folks who behave in appreciative, familiar, undemanding ways. They leave because they find their Global Majority collaborators challenging (for instance: "They were too angry" or "They keep assuming I'm racist when they are the ones with the problem" or "They're not nonviolent enough"). Ending the collaboration because of another's reactivity, especially when they have experienced greater impact by the form of oppression you're addressing, is itself a form of reactivity enabled by our privilege.

Urgency is among the challenges that we face when engaged in antiracism work. How can we not feel a sense of urgency, a pressure to act now, when ethnic violence and genocide continue across the world, when Global Majority people continue to experience the profound harm—loss of life, loss of habitat, loss of livelihood, loss of self—that white supremacy culture engenders. At the systemic level we feel urgency to find and implement strategies that can end these macroaggressions. At the individual level we feel urgency to show up and model a new possibility. Like reactivity, urgency can also prevent us from being effective in our work.

Both reactivity and urgency can lead us to act from a place of disconnection from our values. With the desire for speed that reactivity and urgency prompt, we are liable to fall back on deeply implanted behavioral patterns and strategies—that likely have embedded in them the very white supremacy culture and practices we seek to change. From a place of reactivity and urgency, we might turn to moralistic judgments of good/bad and a reliance on punishment and shaming to motivate behavior. We may be less likely to take the time to try to understand the needs that are motivating the behavior that impacted us, and craft a response that addresses the behavior but does not hold with care the ultimate goal of building Beloved Community.

One unfortunately common effect of responding with reactivity and urgency in our antiracism work is shifting focus from centering the needs of the Global Majority people and groups we wish to support to responding only to spur-of-the-moment situations. This happens regardless of our identity as Global Majority or white. Something happens, and from reactivity we rush to condemn the Actor. We may feel urgency: "I need to demonstrate that I don't condone this Actor's behavior, that I'm not racist." Strategies are selected, often without consulting the Receiver to see what they need. Choices on how to move forward are made from that sense of urgency, often grounded in what we value without consideration for what the Receiver needs. We might take action, even as the Receiver, from a place of partial self-connection, without care for the pace and activities that would most support us.

We can respond to reactivity and urgency by slowing down. We can identify, when we are not in the reactive moments, the steps we wish to follow when we are stimulated, when we feel urgency. Who will be our support network? Who can we turn to for support and care, to help us understand what we need before we take action? We may wish to respond to feelings of reactivity or urgency with a needs assessment. This can be done individually or in community. Pause for empathy or self-empathy. Let our reactivity and our urgency make us aware there are needs that have to be understood and take time to identify them *before* acting. What are the specific issues we want to address? What are the needs that are unmet, and for whom? Who needs care? Who needs to grieve? When we release our sense of urgency, when we let our reactivity become a guide rather than a demand, we can move forward in ways that attend to needs for all, including everyone's needs for care, choice, and inclusion.

JOURNALING PROMPT
### The Cost of Urgency and Reactivity

Think of a situation where you're feeling a strong negative reaction and some urgency to act. Reflect and write about what is stimulated when you consider strategically slowing down to be at full choice in your response to racist behavior? Who do you think slowing down will harm, and why? What needs would go unmet for them? And, thinking of times when you acted out of urgency or reactivity, journal about the unmet needs, if any, that resulted for you or others.

As you consider both sets of unmet needs—those from waiting to act and those from acting with urgency, what do you feel is true now? How would you want to proceed? Are there actions you can take to minimize harms arising from either choice?

_____

_____

_____

_____

_____

_____

### *The Tyranny of Intensity*

Another manifestation of white supremacy culture blocks transformative antiracist conversation by prioritizing care for white people's distress. White supremacy culture values the well-being of white people above all other people. If a white person is distressed, as might result when any of the connection blocks are tripped, the expectation arising out of white supremacy culture is that the focus will immediately shift toward relieving that distress. A white person who cries when experiencing shame or guilt, or who expresses fear in the face of a Global Majority person's upset, must be assuaged.

In many settings, white tears or anguish immediately draws the attention of many Global Majority and white persons witnessing them. Some people feel great discomfort when faced with white distress and move to reassure the white person. Others feel anger and attack the white person for their upset. In both cases the attention has shifted to responding to the experience of the white person and de-centers the experience of the Global Majority person.

### WORKSHEET
## Unpacking Our Response to Intensity

Think of a conversation about racism you witnessed or took part in during which others responded with emotional intensity. If you don't have an example of a conversation on racism, choose any conversation with emotional intensity that involved others.

What did you tell yourself about the person who was displaying intensity?

_____

_____

_____

What did you tell yourself about the others who were present?

_____

_____

_____

What was your reaction to the intensity? Did you retreat? If so, look at the "Feelings" and the "Needs and Values" charts in the Appendix (Figures 5 and 6). What were you feeling? What needs were stimulated for you?

_____

_____

_____

Did you get angry? To whom did you direct your anger?

_____

_____

_____

Did you take action to reduce the intensity? What did you do? To whom was your action directed?

_____

_____

_____

Do you notice any patterns about whom you were openhearted toward and whom you judged?

_____

_____

_____

## COMMON BLOCKS **to Connection**
## Defensiveness and Denial

Another way we can show up is with defensiveness. When our actions impact another person, we ideally want to show up with curiosity and care as doing so can enable the Receiver to express more easefully about their experience and for us to generate strategies to attend to any harm. Despite our intentions to show up in this way, many of us find it difficult. In order to avoid feelings of guilt or shame, we might resist any effort to bring our attention to the impact of our actions or to invite repair. We insist on discussing our intentions, as if the purity of our motivations shields us from having to acknowledge any impact. We may attack the person trying to call us in ("This is only a problem because you're hypersensitive about race. You always think everything is a problem").

Many Actors resist empathizing with the Receiver. We believe empathy equals agreement. If we empathize with the impact the Receiver reports, we think we are tacitly admitting that we stimulated the Receiver's pain and were therefore wrong/bad. As we learn to reject dualistic thinking, we can reject the belief "If you are right and good, I must be wrong and bad. If I'm right and good, you must be wrong and bad." When we hold the nuanced position that both the Actor and the Receiver are capable of behaving in ways that meet needs and ways that don't, as the Actor, we can choose to empathize with both ourselves and with the Receiver.

We also want to recall the impact of cognitive bias and social location on perception. We don't have to insist that our observations are the only true ones if we understand that people's perceptions of the same event can vary widely; each person has a different experience. With this understanding, we can access genuine curiosity about the Receiver's perspective. If we don't trust our perspective is understood and the Receiver is not curious about our experience, we can turn to ourselves for self-empathy and acknowledgment. We can also attempt to get our needs to be met by people who are not as stimulated as the Receiver. Bystanders can help. They can choose to listen to the Actor's experience, away from the Receiver, as a contribution to both the Actor and the Receiver. By doing so, the Bystander can help the Receiver access choice in how much they attempt to hold the Actor when the Receiver needs support or space to regroup. The Bystander also supports the Actor's trust that their experience and perspective matters.

### JOURNALING PROMPT
### Unpacking Defensiveness

Think of a time when you were told you impacted someone and felt defensive. Write down what happened and how you responded. What thoughts did you have about the situation that contributed to your defensiveness? Consider completing the sentence "If I acknowledge I (*describe action*) and it impacted the Receiver by (*describe the Receiver's impact*), it would mean (*I am...or they are...*). Write the feelings and needs that are stimulated for you as you complete those sentences. Consider how holding this belief serves you. What is it protecting? What do you lose by believing it? What would you gain or lose if you let this belief go?

_____

_____

_____

_____

_____

_____

## COMMON BLOCKS to Connection: Prioritizing Process over Content

Another insidious block to connection endemic to white supremacy culture is the insistence on a specific form or way we engage in dialogue over the content of the dialogue itself. Prioritizing process and rules over content can effectively silence people who are trying to engage in discussion over real harm. When the process is constructed unilaterally by those in power and favors a way of interacting typical of the ones with power, it can be difficult for disempowered people to find a path to engage.

In one disheartening example, two Black men attended a Nonviolent Communication retreat for the first time. Their attempts to ask the white facilitator how Nonviolent Communication could be used to address power inequities were met with a process request: "Can you ask that using the observation, feelings, needs, request format?" It's hard to imagine the facilitator needed this format to understand the content of the men's question. They asked again. The trainer's refusal to respond unless their question was in the specified format was repeated. The men became increasingly agitated, their voices rising. The facilitator justified his request that they follow the Nonviolent Communication structure by stating he did not trust the men were really interested in his answer because of their intensity. Ultimately these men left the retreat.

In this example the facilitator insisted on the men following his rules (rules he set that they did not yet know) before he would engage in their content. His prioritization of process successfully silenced people seen as a potential threat and secured the facilitator's comfort. It is important to recognize that for some conversations, especially ones about race, just having the conversation breaks an implicit rule. When the Florida legislature banned schools from discourse that taught about historical racism that they argued might stimulate feelings of guilt or shame, it essentially codified a white supremacist culture belief that conversations about the harms of racism were not permissible.[45] There is no process within white supremacy culture that could make a conversation about such content tenable, so the content itself is not allowed.

WORKSHEET
## Unpacking the Focus on Process

Have you had or witnessed a disagreement with someone from a racial or ethnic group different from your own, especially one that did not end well? Briefly describe that conversation. What was the content? Did you discuss the content—the issue—or did the conversation become a tug-of-war over process?

_____

_____

_____

Were there things the person said or did that were uncomfortable for you to experience? (It may have been the intensity with which they spoke, the topic, or even the timing and circumstances of the conversation.)

_____

_____

_____

How did you respond? Note especially any dualistic thinking (such as, "They're wrong for saying/doing that").

_____

_____

_____

As you reflect on your response, look at the "Feelings" and the "Needs and Values" charts in the Appendix (Figures 5 and 6). What feelings did you experience? For each feeling, determine what need might have stimulated that feeling.

---

---

---

 **NEUROSCIENCE CONCEPT**
**Our Brains as Gatekeepers**

In continuation of the discussion of bias in Chapter 5, scientists have identified more than fifty patterns, or cognitive biases, through which our brains tend to block us from relating to the world as it is. The one that we focus on in more detail here is "confirmation bias." This means that the more we believe our position, the less we can let in new information that might change our minds. Our brains simply erase incoming information that contradicts what we understand. We can even see the erasure happening in fMRIs, which are brain images that show blood flow.[46] In other words, the more we believe our position, the less able we are to change our minds and let in new information.

In systemic racism the way confirmation bias works is that a person with privilege is confident that they are the center of the world. In this confidence that they know and understand the world as it is, and that they have rightfully earned their position, their brains simply discount and erase any new information about the harms of systemic racism. Confirmation bias is a tragic, built-in, human neural conservatism that prevents us from taking action on all global issues of inequality, including systemic racism and the climate crisis. Fortunately, once we understand what is happening, we become more able to integrate new information, reduce the harm we do, and work to change the world.

**JOURNALING PROMPT**
## Being Able to Take in New Information

All of us toggle between being able to see the big picture of the harmful systems within which we live and losing sight of the harm we are doing systemically. As you consider systemic racism, could you name one of the ways that you are participating in systemic harm? Do you live in a neighborhood that is primarily white with high property values as a result of redlining that gives your children access to higher-quality teachers and education when people in Global Majority neighborhoods with artificially depressed property values do not have such advantages? As you consider global inequality, if you live in the global north, do you upgrade your cell phone every two years, even though the labor and materials that are used to make cell phones are provided by people in the Global South who are often paid far below a living wage, and in some cases are enslaved? How does your consciousness of what is happening and your ability to take in new information wax and wane? What do you notice when you bring this phenomenon to your awareness?

_____

_____

_____

_____

_____

_____

## COMMON BLOCKS to Self-Compassion around Confirmation Bias

The most common block to self-compassion for confirmation bias is our desire not to have any confirmation bias—our longing to be "the exception to the rule"—to go beyond the limits of our human brains and bodies. For people who do not have privilege, this can look like wanting to be able to overcome all the problems of systemic racism individually and not be affected by them, no matter how much historic (and current) oppression has impacted physical health, social cohesion, economic and educational opportunities, and so on for themselves and their families. For people with privilege, this can look like wanting not to be subject to biases and distortions, not wanting to have limited empathy in relationship to those with less privilege, and not wanting to be subject to the tendency to discount new information.

### QUESTIONNAIRE
### Do You Want to Be the Exception to the Rule?

*Give your responses to the following questions points from 0–5 (0 = never, 5 = always):*

_____ How often do you learn about something human brains do, like losing empathy for those with less privilege, and believe that you are different from and generally respond more responsibly than the research subjects?

_____ When you learn something new that contradicts or challenges your sense of yourself in the world, how often do you discount the new information so that you can continue to live as you always have?

_____ When you are reviewing something you did that you regret and that may have caused harm to another, how often do you distract yourself or reframe the incident through the lens of your intention?

____ How often do you think about systemic inequities and then start listing all the ways in which you have no power or privilege, and thus no responsibility, making yourself an exception to collective responsibility?

____ When you are reviewing something you did that you regret and that may have caused harm to another, how often do you imagine making a repair and then start thinking about your own needs in the situation instead and never make the repair?

____ When you are reviewing something you did that you regret and that may have caused harm to another, how often do you revert to family patterns and values, rather than doing something new?

____ How often do you believe you are too small and insignificant to make a difference, so what you do doesn't matter?

____ How often do you minimize new information about harm that the overall collective is inflicting on the Global Majority, so that you can continue to live as you have?

____ How often do you list all the stressful things you are living through rather than making any changes in your life strategies or taking new action to make things better?

____ How often do you have a moment of consciousness about this strategy of believing that we are exceptions rather than taking responsibility as part of the whole, only to have the consciousness sink from view within you like a disappearing island?

____ **TOTAL**

**SCORING:**

**40–50:** First of all, congratulations on your honesty and your self-responsibility. The ability to see the way we make information disappear in order to continue to live our lives as usual is the first step toward Beloved Community. The next is to invite real change and actual action.

**30–39:** Welcome to the gradual awakening, the sense that something is not right and needs to change. The next step is to claim your own significance and mattering.

**20–29:** You've been doing some hard work to be in relationship with reality as it is, and to keep it from slipping away into believing that you are an exception. Thank you for being engaged with the struggle.

**0–19:** Thank you for being with the world as it is. You may already be working quite steadily for change. It's not an easy path. Make sure you give yourself moments of rest and even sometimes pleasure and a little raucous joy. The world needs your joy as well as your work.

It can be challenging to look at confirmation bias and to see all the ways it is at work in our lives to preserve the status quo and keep us functioning within an inequitable system. The primary benefit it serves is to reduce stress for us as mammals, but once we begin to prioritize Beloved Community, it can be more stressful to remain ignorant than it is to really see the world and choose the issues we would like to address.

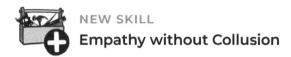

NEW SKILL
## Empathy without Collusion

In November 2022 a common microaggression played out on the world wide stage between Ngozi Fulani, director of a British charity, and Susan Hussey, a longtime member of the British royal entourage.[47] A review of a partial accounting of the conversation between them showed Ms. Hussey asked Ms. Fulani a version of the dreaded question "Where are you really from?" at least eight times despite Ms. Fulani's provision at least three times of information indicating she was born and raised in the UK.[48] You are likely already aware after reading Chapter 8 in this handbook that Ms. Hussey did a classic microaggression of the "You're an Alien in Your Own Land" variety.

Imagine what might have happened next. Friends of Ms. Fulani would circle around her and offer empathy. Friends of Ms. Hussey would likely do the same for her. In situations like this, it can be common for people who believe they are offering empathy to instead offer agreement with their friend's narrative and interpretation of what happened. This agreement is usually positively received since it validates the Receiver's experience. However, this agreement (also known as "colluding with the story") can unconsciously reinforce the Receiver's narrative rather than provide true empathy for the distress, which is separate from agreement about the cause of the distress.

What is the difference? Agreeing with narrative reinforces judgments or interpretations the Receiver (or the person speaking) is sharing. The speaker feels relief because the repetition of their version of events by another person can offer a sense of shared reality, which can serve as a proxy for being understood. True empathy does not seek to affirm any point of view as the true one. Indeed, we can even bypass the details of the story. Our focus in empathy is on the needs and feelings that were stimulated by the event. When feelings and needs are fully reflected, we experience real understanding.

DEMONSTRATION: *Agreement with Narrative*

Here is what agreement with narrative *could* have looked like in an imaginary conversation with Ms. Fulani:

**MS. FULANI:** I can't believe that woman! I didn't even get to talk about Sistah Space. The only thing she cared about was where I was from?! She's completely racist.

**LISTENER:** Yes. That really was racist! Everybody knows that's a loaded question.

**MS. FULANI:** Yeah. Eight times where you're from?! And not a single question about Sistah Space? It's like I and the work I do didn't matter. I was just a puzzle for her to solve.

**LISTENER:** True. It's like you were invisible! She was just running her own script and really didn't care about you.

While Ms. Fulani may feel some relief at the shared agreement between her and the listener, she is not leaving this dialogue with a deeper understanding of what made this so painful beyond the general idea that it was racist. Using even the classic form of feelings and needs empathy in Nonviolent Communication, the listener could respond empathically to Ms. Fulani.

DEMONSTRATION: *Classic Feelings and Needs Empathy*

**MS. FULANI:** I can't believe that woman! I didn't even get to talk about Sistah Space. The only thing she cared about was where I was from?! She's completely racist.

**LISTENER:** Yeah. Are you feeling disheartened because you were so longing to have your work celebrated and to be seen for all of who you are, not just your race?

**MS. FULANI:** Yeah. Eight times where you're from?! And not a single question about Sistah Space? It's like I didn't matter. I was just a puzzle for her to solve.

**LISTENER:** Are you furious because you really wanted choice? And is there some heartbreak because you were so jazzed about the opportunity for recognition and support for your work creating safe space for domestic violence survivors?

Empathic responding could help Ms. Fulani move beyond the surface relief that comes from labeling and judging the racist behavior. Empathy can help Ms. Fulani connect to her longing for celebration and support for her work and to be seen and acknowledged for the complex human being she is. This understanding of her needs can lead to strategies, both for repair from the Palace and for Ms. Fulani to reach for to meet those needs.

WORKSHEET
## From Collusion to Empathy

As with Receivers, we also want to respond to Actors with empathy rather than collude with their narrative. As Actors, notice when we insist on being seen for our intention, or when we resort to blaming ourselves or judging the Receiver. If someone were to try to educate us or raise our awareness during those moments, they would likely be unsuccessful, as a high level of activation often prevents us from taking in new learning. Instead, when we notice patterns of defensiveness and denial, we can seek out empathy or self-empathy. Receiving empathy can be an important resource that makes it possible for us to trust that we still belong, still matter to others, and can open the door for more difficult conversations. Starting with empathy is equivalent to tilling the field before we plant the seeds of change.

Let's practice this skill by imagining what Ms. Hussey might say, and how a listener could respond. In contrast to colluding, fill in what your empathy guesses might be for what was going on at a deeper level for Ms. Hussey:

**MS. HUSSEY:** I can't believe that woman made such a big deal of this. I was just being polite.


**Colluding with Narrative:** Right, you were even showing interest in her background. What could possibly be impolite about that?

**Your Empathic Response:** _____

_____

_____

_____

_____

_____

**MS. HUSSEY:** When I asked her where she was from, why would she tell me where she worked? I was trying to help her feel comfortable. She could have just answered my question. I don't know what she was trying to accomplish!

**Colluding with Narrative:** So strange she was pretending she didn't know what you were asking. Everybody knows this kind of polite dance. It doesn't mean anything.

**Your Empathic Response:** _____

_____

_____

_____

_____

_____

IN CLOSING
## Addressing Defensiveness with Empathy

In our journey into antiracism—as we unpack reactivity, intensity, and defensiveness—our self-compassion is indispensable. There isn't any way to see the impact that confirmation bias has on us and move forward with confidence unless we are well-supported by self-compassion. And the work of finding empathy for others without colluding with them needs heavy doses of both compassion and self-compassion, while holding our emphasis on Beloved Community, which both inspires us and lightens our load. In Chapter 11 we look at ways to more fully claim our dreams of Beloved Community without shame and move them into commitment.

# 11

# "Calling In" to Support Antiracism Goals

ANTIRACISM CONCEPT
**"Calling In" versus "Calling Out"**

"Calling in" and "calling out" as responses to stop racist behavior and invite change are concepts that have received much public attention. Popular opinion often applies the good/bad binary to calling in and calling out. In some circles calling out is viewed as harsh, aggressive, and disconnecting while calling in is seen as respectful and supportive. In other circles calling in can be deemed as an inauthentic sugarcoating of racism aimed at protecting white fragility while calling out is viewed as an authentic, real expression that values and protects the energy of Global Majority people. Some people working in the field of antiracism differentiate between calling in and calling out by defining its audience: calling in is done privately or in small groups while calling out is done publicly.[49] Others differentiate the two terms by defining the depth and duration of contact.[50]

We find both calling in and calling out share important functions. Both have a primary purpose to interrupt racist behavior. In addition, we see both calling in and calling out as attempts to offer feedback that an impact has happened. In doing so, they both fill a function necessary for positive peace: raising awareness when harm exists. Instead of celebrating one and vilifying the other, we see both calling in and calling out as strategies that meet different needs at different times.

We believe calling out is a powerful repudiation of racial rules that prohibited Global Majority people from complaining about the impact of white supremacy culture. Those calling out center the impact sustained by the Receiver because of white supremacy culture and refuse to let the impact go unacknowledged. In concert with that, there is often clarity by those calling out that any form of authentic expression is welcome, without any demand that it be sanitized or made palatable for those who might witness it. This point of view recognizes the amount of labor Global Majority folks have given to try to have their experience neatly packaged in hopes that it would be more easily understood, acknowledged, and addressed. When calling out, the person who is expressing is doing work. It is labor to express our pain, however raw and unfiltered. The person calling out does not necessarily do *additional* work to make their expression palatable for those witnessing them.

When calling in, people are often willing to take on the extra labor involved to support understanding because of calling in's focus on learning and reflection in order to achieve behavior change. There is an intention to prioritize sufficient connection when calling in so that the information being transmitted is more likely to be received. This may result in labor to clarify terms and make connections between behavior and systems of oppression easier to perceive by those who do not readily see them. It may involve labor for the person doing the calling in to self-regulate and self-empathize both in terms of their reaction to the original stimulus and when they receive reactions from those being called in.

As you can see, both calling in and calling out have a role in creating Beloved Community. If you are the Actor, you can take any attempt to raise your awareness of your impact, no matter how gently or skillfully done, as an invitation for you to check how well your actions are aligning with your values. If you are the Receiver, you can assess how to hold both your needs for expression and being seen, and any hope you have of contributing to a different world. As Bystanders, we can step toward holding both the Actor and the Receiver with care, choosing not to collude with the story or judge the method of delivery, instead serving as a bridge of connection between the two.

NEW SKILL

## Calling In the Actor

We have explored how we could support an Actor or a Receiver with empathy without colluding with their narrative or story of what occurred. While empathy is of crucial importance in releasing us from paradigms of exclusion and inclusion, empathizing without raising awareness of impact and inviting dialogue is another way of maintaining negative peace. In such a case, we are using empathy as a salve that takes the sting away from an injury without treating the underlying problem. Both calling in and calling out are strategies that can raise awareness.

In Chapter 10 we imagined some empathic conversations that might occur with both Ms. Fulani and Ms. Hussey following Ms. Hussey's repeatedly ignoring Ms. Fulani's report that she was born in Britain and insisting on knowing where Ms. Fulani was "really" from. We have seen in the media and can imagine the many forms of calling out of Ms. Hussey that occurred in response to this line of questioning. They could include a simple statement that the line of questioning was racist to calls for her to step down to prevent further harm. What could calling in Ms. Hussey look like? Let's extend our imaginary dialogue to demonstrate.

DEMONSTRATION: *Calling In*

**MS. HUSSEY:** I can't believe that woman made such a big deal of this. I was just being polite.

**BYSTANDER:** I'm guessing you're shocked at the degree of upset? Are you really wishing people had a sense of how much you value making everyone feel welcomed?

**MS. HUSSEY:** Yes, I didn't know anything about her. I was just trying to be nice!

**BYSTANDER:** I really get a sense of how confusing this all is. Are you open to hearing my understanding of why this was so painful?

**MS. HUSSEY:** Of course. I definitely didn't mean anything by it.

**BYSTANDER:** Well, I think one important piece is that I don't believe anyone is saying you were intentionally trying to be racist, but your questions did have a huge impact on Ms. Fulani and those who heard about it.

**MS. HUSSEY:** But why? If people know I wasn't trying to be racist, why can't they just let it go?

**BYSTANDER:** I hear your question and I see that you really want to understand. I appreciate that. (Pause.) My take is that this really touched a deep wound for a lot of people. There is an idea that being British is the same as being white. Anybody who has darker skin or who is Black, Asian, or African—anyone not white—is automatically assumed to be born elsewhere. Even if their family has been here for generations, people still make that assumption, which sends a message you don't really belong here. Can you see why that would be a difficult message for someone to receive?

**MS. HUSSEY:** Well, yes, but I didn't say that, did I? I would have asked anyone where they were from!

**BYSTANDER:** Yes, I get that from your vantage point you might ask that question of anyone, and for you that's just showing interest in the other person. I think what is key in understanding the impact your questions had on her is that as a Black woman, her experience has been quite different from yours as a white person in a society that has been made by white people, built around the views, experiences, and needs of people who are white, whose experiences you share. You've made your way in a world where your sense of belonging and value were never questioned because of your race. You may have been judged and had to prove yourself for other reasons—say, for being a woman—but my guess is that you have never felt shamed or doubted or suspected because you were white. I'd guess you never felt shunned or like you didn't belong in society because of your race. Is that so?

**MS. HUSSEY:** Now that you ask this, I guess I have always felt a part of this society. I haven't had to struggle with race, I don't want anyone to do so. Why can't we just treat everyone like a human being? I am not a bad person.

**BYSTANDER:** I hear that you truly don't want racism to be an issue for anyone, that you want to do good in the world. I trust that intention, I do. And what I really want you to see is that for those who have not been born white and do not automatically fit into the dominant society, a white society, it's a very common experience to not be accepted, to not feel like they belong; to always be seen as "the other." When this happens for so much of their lives, in very hurtful ways, receiving the question "Where are you really from?" lands as just another painful reminder of not belonging.

**MS. HUSSEY:** Oh my! I had not thought of how loaded my question was and the impact it could have; I asked it without considering the pain it could stir up for someone who was not white like myself. I feel somewhat ashamed and embarrassed in having done so. Thank you for saying you trust my intention. That matters to me.

**BYSTANDER:** Yes. And I think there is a real longing for even well-intentioned people who are white to understand this, to carry this awareness of how Black people, how Global Majority people, see and experience things that may be "normal" for a white person but that have very different and negative impacts for them.

## Choosing Our Response

Think of a time when you witnessed a microaggression. What choice did you make in the moment? Think of how you would call them out. What would you say if you wanted to interrupt harm and prioritize full expression of the pain? Write that statement and share the feelings you connect to when you consider saying it. What needs would be met for you and what needs would not be met for you by that calling-out response? Now consider calling them in. What would you say if you wanted to prioritize information about your experience or about the larger social context that might lead to a shift? Write this out. Share the feelings you connect to when you consider saying it. What needs would be met for you, and what needs would not be met for you by that calling-in response?

_____

_____

_____

_____

NEUROSCIENCE CONCEPT **The Instrumental, Relational, and Integrational Brains**

Brains can focus in three different ways. First, the instrumental brain focuses on tasks. Second, the relational brain prioritizes people. Third, the integrational brain keeps its attention on both tasks and relationships, and makes choices about how to proceed based on what we value most. The path of integration lets us stay connected to our longing for Beloved Community—a community where everyone belongs as we are, and where we work for more life-serving systems.

The instrumental and relational brain systems involve different areas of the brain and are fueled by different neurotransmitters.[51] They give us two entirely different feelings about being alive. When we are in the instrumental brain, we want to make people acknowledge the harm they've done, we want to make them pay to balance the scales, we want to call them out, and we want to cast them out if they can't contribute to the struggle. Our goals are more important than people. Our goal of changing the system matters more than the people (including the people we do care about, the people we don't care about, and everyone else) caught up in those systems. When we are in the relational brain, we prioritize and feel our individual relationships and let go of goals. When we are connected to our higher purpose, we can integrate both kinds of wisdom to contribute to our greater vision, staying connected to each person while moving ahead toward Beloved Community.

QUESTIONNAIRE
## Body Sensations and Brain Systems

Invite yourself to think about your to-do list. What are the next three things that you would like yourself to do after you finish this exercise?

_____

_____

_____

And what are the next three actions connected with antiracist action that you would like yourself to take?

_____

_____

_____

How does your body feel when you think about things that need to be done or that you would like yourself to do?

_____

_____

_____

Now think about a warm relationship you have with someone, that is in some way connected with antiracism. What happens with your body sensations?

_____

_____

_____

Now think about a difficult relationship you have with someone, that is in some way connected with antiracism. What happens with your body sensations?

_____

_____

_____

Now sink into your love for Beloved Community, in all its complexity and inclusiveness. What happens with your body sensations?

_____

_____

_____

What action would you like to take based on this love?

_____

_____

_____

What happens with your body now?

_____

_____

_____

What is it like to contrast the simple desire to take action (your to-do list) with your thoughts about relationships? And then what is it like to contrast the first two brain focuses with the desire to take action grounded in your love?

_____

_____

_____

As you reflected in the "Body Sensations and Brain Systems" questionnaire on your body's responses to your different types of brain focus (instrumental, relational, and integrational), you might have noticed the power and calm that come from being with your integrational brain. Knowing what we love and making decisions from that place roots us in our intention and allows nourishment to flow upward to us and to restore our life energy for this journey.

COMMON BLOCKS **to Self-Compassion:**
**Being Shamed for Our Dreams**

Being met with a shaming or humiliating response when we attempt to share our dream for Beloved Community is one of the most common ways that self-compassion becomes blocked. When we share our dreams, they can be met with sarcasm or ridicule. If our dreams for a better world are ridiculed, we often give them up or hide them away and try not to think about them again. One of the most effective ways to remove this kind of block is to Time Travel to the moment when the dream was lost or relinquished and reclaim it for ourselves and for the world.

WORKSHEET
**Time Travel to Reclaim a Dream**

Choose a memory you want to work with. What was the worst moment of shame or humiliation in connection with your dream for a better world?

_____

_____

_____

Identify the age of the self when the memory happened: _____

Consent: Ask the younger self if it's okay to Time Travel to them to bring them empathy and resonance:

☐ Yes ☐ No

If it's not okay with your younger self that we travel to them, ask them if we can try again in a little while. Sometimes it takes some time for trust to develop.

If they say "yes," gather your resonating witness—either the part of you that has warmth for the younger self, or bring someone else along in your imagination who has warmth for the younger self.

Who is your resonating witness? _____

_____

Where are you in the memory? Describe anything you remember about the place.

_____

_____

As you arrive in the memory, visualize the current you, in your grown body, arriving in the past to be with your younger self. Describe the clothes you're wearing right now, and what it would be like for your younger self to see you in them.

_____

_____

_____

Freeze the environment so that everyone is safe. You can put everyone in floating golden bubbles, or airlift people out, or turn them to stone.

What do you do to immobilize or remove everyone else in the memory?

_____

_____

Notice whether your younger self can perceive your presence. (Do they know you are there?)

☐ Yes     ☐ No

If the younger self cannot perceive your presence, make sure to ask about shock, and whether the younger self has stopped breathing. Perception is not absolutely necessary, just helpful.

If the younger self can perceive you, make sure they know who you are (perhaps by introducing yourself). What will you say to introduce yourself and your resonating witness? (For example: "I'm your older self, who loves you. I have come back for you because I don't want you to have to live through this alone. I am here for you.")

_____

_____

_____

Now notice the body experience of the younger self related to what is happening in the memory. Based on what you feel or perceive, what is the first thing that your younger self would appreciate having acknowledged?

- Have you stopped breathing?
- Do you wish you could fall through the floor? Or that others would fall through the floor?
- Would you appreciate a little acknowledgment of shock? Or total bone-deep fatigue?
- How about helplessness or hopelessness?
- How about other emotions?
  - Is there any sorrow?
  - Is there any alarmed aloneness?
  - Is there any fear?
  - Is there any anger?
  - And strange though it may be to ask, is there any disgust?
- Do you need to live in a world where dreams are celebrated and valued?

What is a metaphorical description of what happened to your dream in this moment? Did it fracture, shrivel, disappear, go far away, or something else? Can you pick it back up and heal it or bring it back to wholeness?

_____

_____

_____

What else would you like to acknowledge for your younger self? What else does your younger self need acknowledged?

_____

_____

_____

_____

_____

_____

How does your younger self respond? What happens with your younger self's body sensations?

_____

_____

_____

_____

_____

_____

Once the body of your younger self relaxes fully, invite them and your dream back home to present time with you. Would they like to come?

☐ Yes　　　☐ No

If they would not like to come, set them up with protection, or safety, or another place to be where they can feel good. Describe this situation or place.

_____

_____

_____

If they would like to come, step back through time and space, and bring them home and fully celebrate their presence in your present.

Now that you have your earlier self either in a safe place or home with you, how do you feel about your dream? Often people start to see their experience differently after a Time Travel. Is anything different for you?

_____

_____

_____

### ANTIRACISM CONCEPT
## Focus on Impact before Intention

As we have noted, an Actor's defensiveness and denial—often marked by a focus on their intention—is a common response when told that they had an impact on someone. The phrase "Impact before Intention" is often used to remind the Actor that when they choose to attend to the impact the Receiver sustained before (and sometimes without) focusing on their intention, the Receiver often gains a sense that their experience matters and is being held with care. However, many Actors struggle with what this means. What is one supposed to do when asked to focus on impact before intention, and why does it truly matter?

When we focus on impact, we hope to let the Receiver know that their perspective and experience, even if not shared by us, matters. In doing so, we acknowledge with humility that there is likely to be a difference in perspective between people who share different social locations. We are acknowledging that even if the impact is far removed from our experience and intent, the fact that it happened matters and the impact sustained by the Receiver matters. One way to show this is to empathize with all the layers of impact that occurred. Our Observation Iceberg model can offer some guidance on levels of reflection (Figure 4).

You have already practiced making observations at the external, internal, and systemic levels. As the Receiver speaks about their impact, the Actor can listen for information that will show what level the Receiver is talking about. The Actor can then offer feelings and needs guesses or other forms of reflection relevant to that level.

 WORKSHEET **Practice Roleplay of Offering Empathy for Impact**

Think of a time when you committed or saw a microaggression. You will be practicing from the viewpoint of the Actor, so choose a situation where you are open to embodying the Actor.

Briefly describe the situation.

_____

_____

_____

*Observe*                                                    *Respond*

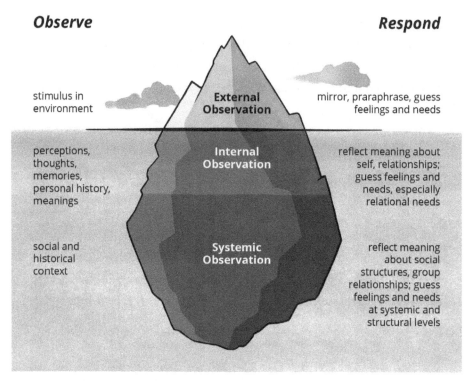

**FIGURE 4. Levels of Reflection**
© Mireille van Bremen and Roxy Manning

What did the Receiver say in the situation that expressed their pain? If they did not speak to it, what would you imagine they might say to express their pain about the action?

_____

_____

_____

Think about what you would say to address the impact of your action using the model (refer to Figure 4 as needed). If you find that you are too upset to think clearly, offer yourself some functional self-empathy—that is, connect just enough to how you are feeling and what is important to you in the situation (your needs and values) to help you come back to presence with the Receiver.

Write out a line of functional self-empathy.

"When the Receiver expressed _____,
*(name the observation that occurred)*

I felt _____
*(name the feeling)*

because _____
*(scan the "Needs and Values" chart in the Appendix (Figure 6) and choose one your body responds to)*

is important to me."

Next, think about what you would say to offer empathy to the Receiver, attending to as many layers of stimulus that you can determine. As illustrated in Figure 4, at the external level you would mirror, paraphrase, and guess feelings and needs. Write out a line of empathy at this level:

_____

_____

_____

At the systemic level you would reflect meaning about social structures and group relationships, as well as guess feelings and needs at systemic and structural levels. Here's an example.

**A RECEIVER OF THE "ALIEN IN MY OWN LAND" MICRO-AGGRESSION MIGHT SAY:** "It's so scary when people don't see me as American. Don't you get how dangerous this is! As soon as there's any problem, it's the Black and Brown folks who get locked up or even killed. Look what happened with the Japanese in World War II and all the Muslim folks (and even non-Muslim Brown folks) after 9/11."

**A GUESS FOR MEANING MIGHT BE:** "When you see me and other people unconsciously linking ethnic origin to belonging as Americans, and you recall the patterns of scapegoating during times of unrest, are you terrified thinking the conditions still exist for it to happen again?"

**A FEELINGS AND NEEDS GUESS AT THIS SYSTEMIC LEVEL MIGHT BE:** "Are you longing for full acknowledgment of your identity and that of other Global Majority US folks as full members of the United States? Are you feeling anguish because you desperately want protection and stability for all communities, regardless of race or ethnic origin?"

Write out a line of empathy at the systemic level for your situation:

_____

_____

_____

If the person expressed pain related to their internal experience (personal history, thoughts, memories, meanings, perceptions), you can also reflect meaning about self and relationships as well as guess feelings and needs, especially relational needs. (If the person has not expressed themselves at this level, take care since guesses about internal experience can often fall into stereotyping and thus further harm.) Write out a line of empathy at the internal level (if in response to something the Receiver shared):

_____

_____

_____

As we empathize with a Receiver who has been impacted by us, it's likely that we will encounter a few roadblocks. This process requires an intention to hold ourselves with care, even as we open fully to the impact. The capacity to self-empathize even while tuning in to the Receiver is crucial. With practice, we may notice moments of disconnection or self-judgment arising as we hear the Receiver and be able to quickly self-empathize then return fully to the Receiver without interrupting the flow of empathy to the Receiver. If we are not yet able to do so, ask for a break.

When asking for a break, be transparent: "I notice I've got some self-judgment coming up, and I don't want it to get in the way of being open to hearing more about how this was for you. Could we take a five-minute break while I empathize with myself to return to full presence?" Transparency supports the Receiver in trusting that we're not taking a break because we're disgusted or otherwise upset by what they are sharing. It provides clarity the break is a strategy for self-care. During that break we can work with any shame or other self-judgments. Remember that each of these are attempts to raise awareness of something that is important to us. We can try to identify the need or value that the feeling connects to as a way of releasing enough of the tension we feel and returning to choice about hearing the Receiver.

Another potential roadblock occurs when we share our vulnerability with the Receiver with a hope (often unconscious) that they may be moved to reassure us. Receivers may be willing to do so—remember, many Global Majority people have been conditioned to extend care to Actors at cost to themselves. If feelings of vulnerability are strong, the Actor may consider taking a longer break to seek empathy from another, in addition to self-empathy.

IN CLOSING

## Reclaiming Your Dreams

If we want to commit to creating Beloved Community—if that is the dream that most inspires us—we are starting to have the tools for it in our hands. We have the approach of Authentic Dialogue, we're gaining models for using Authentic Dialogue in many different situations, and we know ways of holding care for impact at all levels. Plus, we have actually reclaimed our dream from wherever we had it stowed away for safety. Our last piece of work is connecting to hope, which we explore in Chapter 12 .

# 12

# Engagement Changes Everything

ANTIRACISM CONCEPT
## Fanning the Flame of Hope

An exercise I, Roxy, enjoy asking people to do in workshops is to reflect on someone who inspires you. I choose cards from the Civil Rights Movement deck that show images of people from the 1960s Civil Rights era and summarize what they did.[52] I ask everyone to choose and read a card, then in their own words, share with someone else what they learned about that person. We then discuss the question: "What made it possible for the person depicted on the card to do what they did, especially living in a context where the explicit narrative was that Black people were powerless and inferior."

This question is about hope. What makes it possible for people to give everything, including their lives, for change when there is little evidence that real change is possible? My students consistently identify qualities they gleaned from the stories of the Civil Rights pioneers that are essential for hope. First, we must have vision. If all we can imagine is what we are currently mired in, there is no hope. Hope is not an anemic wish for something to be different. It is grounded in a sense of what we are reaching for, what is possible. When I can envision a different way of being, of interacting, of living, then I can hope for it. Beloved Community is that vision—it inspires us to imagine a world where everyone has what they need to thrive. A world where white supremacy culture no longer holds sway. A world where society recognizes and celebrates all beings. Where we can show up in our full, naturally imperfect humanity in trust that we will receive loving feedback to support healthy connections with each other.

We also identify other characteristics of people who have acted from hope. Just as we need a vision of what will be, we need the capacity to acknowledge what was and is and to grieve. Mourning takes courage. It requires us to be willing to experience our heartbreak, witness our pain. It requires us to trust that we will not become overwhelmed and immobilized by our grief. Instead, our grief can replenish us. Our ability to acknowledge what we have lost, while maintaining our vision of what can be, can provide the fuel that energizes us.

We need trust in ourselves and our capacity, trust that is internal, grounded in our knowing of ourselves and not in external judgments. We need resilience. We need willingness to risk, to fail, and to try again. When we can see our failures as the result of temporary limits in resources and capacity rather than a signpost of our wrongness, we are more able to keep trying, to keep reaching for our goal. Most of all, we need community. Human beings are interdependent. We are at our best when we build loving relationships of mutual support, relationships in which we each take turns doing the work that is necessary and resting when we need. We need relationships in which we can share our pain and receive support in healing, relationships in which we can authentically share our dreams and our fears, and celebrate and mourn them together. In such community we can find hope.

JOURNALING PROMPT
## Mourning as Fuel for Hope

White supremacy culture and its practices result in loss for all of us, Global Majority and white. What is a loss you have experienced stemming from white supremacy culture? Write down this loss, as specifically as possible. As you reflect on this loss, allow yourself to connect to your emotions. Notice whatever emerges—grief, fear, anger, numbness. Allow yourself to feel that emotion. Where do you feel it? Write down what you notice. You might complete the sentences: When I think of the absence of _____, I feel _____. When I think of losing _____, I feel _____. When I realize I am unable to _____, I feel _____.

Now reflect on the need that is underneath the feeling. What needs would be met for you if you had access to the thing that you lost? Explore the need fully. As you journal, reflect on what this need means for you. How do you imagine feeling if that need were met? How could having this need met enrich your life? End this reflection by considering what needs would be met for you if you found another way to cultivate this need.

_____

_____

_____

_____

_____

_____

NEUROSCIENCE CONCEPT
## Hope and Measured Optimism

Research shows us that hope is absolutely necessary for well-being. Feeling hope creates foundational resilience for our immune systems and keeps us engaged—in life, in relationships, and in the long commitment to social justice. But it can be hard to maintain feelings of hope in the face of a large-scale, centuries-long system of oppression like systemic racism.

When hope is active in us, it supports us to do two things: plan to meet our goals and move toward them with determination. Surprisingly, we can actually see hope in fMRI scans of human brains. When people experience the sensation of hope, they have more gray matter volume (the neurons we use to think) in the left supplementary motor cortex—an area used to take action.[53] Hope gives us agency, engagement, and well-being—all of which are vital characteristics for the creation of an antiracist world.

We live in a world filled with cynicism, which is hope's antimatter. Some people even say that cynicism is their religion. Cynicism is a very compelling perspective, because it protects against heartbreak and lets people keep moving in a world where their dreams have been lost. Perhaps it is helpful to learn that while it seems that cynicism is a salve for heartache and disappointment, it actually does not improve our immune system's responses nor lift us out of depression. It does not support us, on a neurochemical level, the way that hope can.

Measured optimism isn't about simply feeling better: it's about nourishing our brains to have the energy to live in alignment with our values. This plays a pivotal role in our capacity to bring about the world in which we wish to live. And yet, we are surrounded by unconscious contracts, other people's as well as our own, which tell us not to have hope. With these unconscious contracts we are doing our best to avoid the crash of continual disappointment. So for folks who have made a home in cynicism as a way to survive: How can we enable a shift into a place of hope? Let's take a moment to write about hope. Are you resistant? Do you protest? Are you curious? Are you eager?

 JOURNALING PROMPT **The Journey of Hope and Self-Compassion in Antiracism**

How did people express hope or respond to it in your childhood family? What needs do you believe were met by that response? What are some beliefs you now have about hope at your current age? How do those beliefs serve you? What impact do they have on your self-compassion?

_____

_____

_____

_____

_____

_____

_____

Lack of self-compassion is a huge block to hope. Without self-compassion, people might believe that they don't deserve to have hope. Their disgust for themselves, or for the world, might be so constant that there is no place for hope to reside. Without self-compassion, hope can feel like an impossibility.

**QUESTIONNAIRE**
## Feelings and Hope

This questionnaire helps you explore what may be blocking you from hope. Using the "Feelings" chart in the Appendix (Figure 5), choose the words that best describe your emotions.

When I hear that hope is essential for the good functioning of my immune system and my motivation, I feel…

_____

When I think about next month, I feel…

_____

When I think about the future in general, I feel…

_____

When I reach for hope about ending systemic racism, I feel…

_____

When I imagine myself as a hopeful person, I feel…

_____

When I hear that hope is key in giving me agency and helping me find a way forward, I feel…

_____

When I think about my children's children (or the children of today's children), I feel…

_____

When I say to myself, "I have hope," I feel…

_____

When I ask myself to look at myself with compassion, I feel…

_____

When I think about everything I'd like myself to do, I feel…

_____

When I think about humanity as a whole, I feel…

_____

When I think about myself as part of humanity, I feel…

_____

What kinds of feelings do you have? Are they all from the list of feelings that occur when needs are unmet? Or do you have some met-needs feelings too? If all your feelings are connected with needs not being met, it is likely that there is some despair that needs to be acknowledged before you can move forward into hope, no matter how good hope is for you.

### WORKSHEET
### Acknowledging Despair

Review your "Feelings and Hope" questionnaire. Is hope something you feel every day? Or only on special occasions? Do you deserve to have hope? If hope is rare for you, there may be some unconscious contracts getting in your way. Let's look at some of the unconscious contracts that can block hope. Do any of these sound familiar?

- I will not hope.
- I will not let myself have hope.
- I will not believe I deserve to hope.
- I will believe I am too (damaged, wounded, small-minded, broken-hearted, etc.) to be able to hope.

- I will believe that hope is impossible.
- I will believe that hope is stupid.
- I will believe that hope is deluded.
- I will believe that hope is for the innocent.
- I will believe that hope is for everyone else.

### EXERCISE  Releasing Unconscious Contracts That Block Hope

I, (YOUR NAME HERE), promise myself that:
*(Choose one of the hope-negating contracts that seemed true for you from the preceding "Acknowledging Despair" worksheet.)*

Then follow the "General Worksheet to Release Unconscious Contracts" to release any of the contracts that you identified.

With more hope we have more of a capacity to reach out for support. This takes us to our newest skill—calling in support.

### NEW SKILL
### Building Resilience by Calling in Support

As you have seen throughout this handbook, the work of choosing Authentic Dialogues requires us to know ourselves, know our values, and trust that life is better served when we show up fully, expressing our truth and opening to others. We cannot do this work alone. Instead, imagine each of us is a giant coastal redwood tree. Our grounding in the goal of Beloved Community might be shallow, like the roots of the coastal redwood trees. But like those giants, we can reach our roots out toward each other, with each new connection growing our strength. The intertwined roots of the redwoods help them survive strong storms.[54] Similarly, when we join together in community, we can withstand the storm of resistance we encounter as we work to dismantle white supremacy culture. We can connect to our community to help us light up our vision when we lose our way. We can lean into others for authentic feedback about how well our actions align with our values. We can brainstorm together to identify and supply each other with what is needed as we keep paving the road to Beloved Community.

 JOURNALING PROMPT **Envisioning and Accessing Beloved Community**

In Chapter 1 you were invited to journal about your vision of Beloved Community. We'd like you to read what you wrote. If you did not do that journaling activity, take a moment to complete it now before continuing.

Next, write down what resources you can gather now that will support you in moving toward that vision. For each resource you identify, think of a strategy—a person you can speak to, a practice you can adopt—that would help you access that resource. As you end, consider strategies for continued reflection and engagement with these concepts, to support growth and an intentional recommitment to your dream of Beloved Community.

_____

_____

_____

_____

_____

_____

JOURNALING PROMPT
## What This Handbook Has Meant to You

What are your feelings about the future and your place in antiracism now? Have your feelings changed? What has this handbook meant to you? Have the skills of Authentic Dialogue given you any more options for your antiracism work?

_____

_____

_____

_____

_____

_____

## CONCLUSION

We come to the end of this handbook with both celebration and mourning. The thought and action exercises we have offered here in the form of questionnaires, worksheets, and journaling prompts, when practiced and applied, can change brains. Utilizing the transformative capacity of Authentic Dialogue offers us all new models and options for response during difficult or charged encounters. Our hope is that it can also provide new openings for everyone into self-compassion for those times when responding is less available. We hope that these tools are helpful for both Global Majority folks and white folks, as we all navigate the difficulties of maneuvering in a world built on white supremacist ideology and finding our way to Beloved Community.

You are welcome, and encouraged, to return to any of the exercises in this handbook throughout your lifelong journey of antiracism. There will always be unconscious contracts, vulnerability-blocking shame, and unconscious bias to excavate, reveal, and release. When we reject white supremacy culture from any standpoint, we also reject the ethos of perfectionism that reinforces it. Allow yourself to make mistakes, allow yourself to show up differently than you expected, allow yourself to be in process. Have self-compassion when you don't want to act. And push yourself past your comfort zone. Have self-compassion when you feel uncomfortable asking for Authentic Dialogue and you do it anyway. Notice the things that you have been shielded from noticing. Flex your hope: it is how you will stay energized, determined, and healthy.

The research of Patricia G. Devine and colleagues gives us a lot of hope that a reduction of the unconscious perpetuation of white supremacy ideology, through the integration of the knowledge and practices of this handbook, is possible.[55] We hope that the tools in this handbook can support all of us as we work to unlearn cognitive racism and repattern our brains for justice. Devine and colleagues discovered that for people's brains to significantly change their reliance on implicit bias, a number of things need to be in place. The very first is the effort that you put into finding, reading, and working with this handbook. Second, as people who hold the value of Beloved Community, we must be aware of our biases and we must be concerned about the impact of our biases on others. Third, we must want our brains to work differently, be willing to learn about white supremacy culture and implicit bias, and put the effort into tasks and explorations that move our brains away from prejudice. And finally, we need examples of other ways to respond—ways to replace our biased responses with aligned actions that support Beloved Community.

Here are the changes that we envision happening as people of all racial backgrounds integrate the work we are learning in this handbook:

- Everyone, Global Majority and white, replaces their stereotypical responses with nonstereotypical responses. This requires noticing microaggressions, crafting and carrying out repairs, and reaching for vulnerability and personal connection over and over again, instead of lapsing into the easy-on-the-brain but hard-on-Global Majority generalizations or assumptions that do harm.

- White people develop new individual and positive responses to and predictions about Global Majority folks. This is helped by white people having more connection and contact with people who are not white—this contact naturally arises from greater comfort and social imagination, and comes about because of greater intentionality about meeting, speaking with, inviting, and seeking out Global Majority voices.

- Global Majority folks, in connection with their longing for Beloved Community, get to acknowledge truth and trauma, to experience validation of the health and well-being impacts of white supremacy ideology, and to claim new confidence and fierceness in speaking up and taking action, while accompanying themselves and others with self-compassion and compassion.

- An increase in everyone's capacity to see and value the perspective and experience of Global Majority people. On an individual level, Global Majority people increase their trust in their experience mattering to other Global Majority and white people. And white people start to notice when they observe microaggressions being done by themselves or other white people, and to act to mitigate the harm being done. On the systemic level, everyone has a deeper ability to understand and feel strongly about harm being done to the Global Majority, and to act where before they may have assumed their voice did not matter or that the lack of direct impact exempted them from action.

As we come to the end of our handbook, which contains so much love, encouragement, and care for each of you, Roxy and Sarah welcome you to the community of people who are working toward Beloved Community. The vision of Beloved Community has stretched long before us through every human who ever noticed the harmful impact of racism and wanted the world to be better. We invite each of you to continue to learn, integrate, and act in new ways that value every being, knowing these collective actions will challenge the pervasive patterns of white supremacy culture and bring us all closer to the full manifestation of Beloved Community.

# APPENDIX

When needs are
*met*...

When needs are
*unmet*...

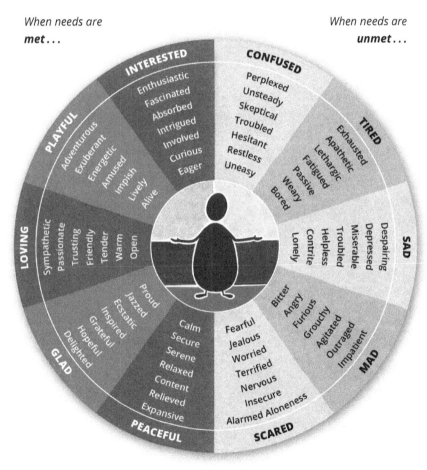

**FIGURE 5. Feelings**
© Mireille van Bremen and Roxy Manning

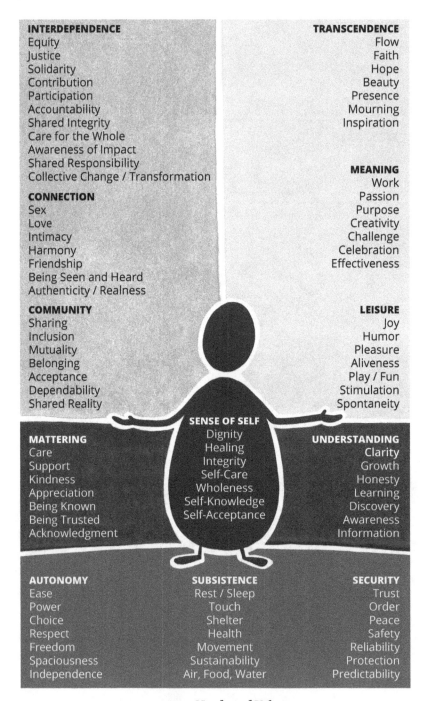

**FIGURE 6. Needs and Values**

© Mireille van Bremen and Roxy Manning

# NOTES

## INTRODUCTION

1. Ibram X. Kendi, *How to Be an Antiracist* (New York: One World, 2019), 19.

2. Kendi, *How to Be an Antiracist*, 105.

3. Rosemary M. Campbell-Stephens, *Educational Leadership and the Global Majority: Decolonising Narratives* (Cham, Switzerland: Springer Nature, 2021), 7.

4. "'Nobody's Free until Everybody's Free': Speech Delivered at the Founding of the National Women's Political Caucus, Washington, DC, July 10, 1971," in *The Speeches of Fannie Lou Hamer: To Tell It Like It Is*, edited by Maegan Parker Brooks and Davis W. Houck (Jackson, MS: 2010; Mississippi Scholarship Online, March 20, 2014), https://doi.org/10.14325/mississippi/9781604738223.003.0017 (accessed November 23, 2022).

5. David J. Kelly, Paul C. Quinn, Alan M. Slater, Kang Lee, Alan Gibson, Michael Smith, Liezhong Ge, and Olivier Pascalis, "Three-Month-Olds, but Not Newborns, Prefer Own-Race Faces," *Developmental Science* 8, no. 6 (2005), https://doi.org/10.1111/j.1467-7687.2005.0434a.x.

6. Kendi, *How to Be An Antiracist*, 9.

7. Roxy Manning, *How to Have Antiracist Conversations: Embracing Our Full Humanity to Challenge White Supremacy* (Oakland, CA: Berrett-Koehler, 2023).

8. Manning, *How to Have Antiracist Conversations.*

## CHAPTER 1

*Epigraph*: Martin Luther King Jr., "Nonviolence: The Only Road to Freedom," *Ebony* (October 1966): 30.

9. The phrase Beloved Community, popularized by Dr. Martin Luther King Jr., is commonly attributed to the metaphysical philosopher Josiah Royce and has

been used to describe an aspirational goal in spiritual communities of diverse faiths as well as secular ones. The vision of Beloved Community is one that has existed and appealed to humans across many times and cultures. See Thich Nhat Hanh, "Sangha and The Beloved Community," excerpt from *Art of Suffering Retreat | Third Dharma Talk at Blue Cliff Monastery*, August 28, 2013 (Pine Bush, NY: Plum Village App), https://www.youtube.com/watch?v=idHSeRRTQ_8/ (accessed November 27, 2022); and Kelly A. Parker and Scott Pratt, "Josiah Royce," *Stanford Encyclopedia of Philosophy*, Stanford University, January 14, 2022, https://plato.stanford.edu/entries/royce/.

10. Martin Luther King Jr., "Letter from Birmingham Jail [King, Jr.]," African Studies Center, University of Pennsylvania, https://www.africa.upenn.edu/Articles_Gen/Letter_Birmingham.html (accessed November 26, 2022).

11. Ibram X. Kendi, *Stamped from the Beginning: The Definitive History of Racist Ideas in America* (New York: Bold Type Books, 2017).

12. Christian Paz, "The Los Angeles City Council's Racist Recording Scandal, Explained," *Vox*, October 19, 2022, https://www.vox.com/policy-and-politics/23404926/los-angeles-city-council-racist-recording-scandal-explained.

13. Stephen W. Porges, "The Polyvagal Theory: New Insights into Adaptive Reactions of the Autonomic Nervous System," *Cleveland Clinic Journal of Medicine* 76, no. 4 suppl. 2 (April 2009), S86–90, https://doi.org/10.3949/ccjm.76.s2.17.

14. "FNS—Elder Teachings by Napos," University of Wisconsin–Green Bay, February 28, 2011, https://youtu.be/LK5Et8MJJJA. National Institutes of Health, "Medicine Ways: Traditional Healers and Healing," US National Library of Medicine, https://www.nlm.nih.gov/nativevoices/exhibition/healing-ways/medicine-ways/medicine-wheel.html (accessed October 2022).

15. Bettina Elias Siegel, "Shaming Children So Parents Will Pay the School Lunch Bill," *New York Times*, May 1, 2017, https://www.nytimes.com/2017/04/30/well/family/lunch-shaming-children-parents-school-bills.html.

16. Eknath Easwaran, *Gandhi the Man: The Story of His Transformation*, 3rd edition (Tomales: Nilgiri Press, 2011), 53.

## CHAPTER 2

17. Kendi, *Stamped from the Beginning*, esp., 22–46.

18. Cheryl I. Harris, "Whiteness as Property," *Harvard Law Review* 106, no. 8 (1993): 1709–1791, 1725, https://doi.org/10.2307/1341787.

19. Myisha V. Cherry, "Breaking Racial Rules through Rage," Reynolds Lecture, Learning on Demand, Elon University, April 2019, https://blogs.elon.edu/ondemand/breaking-racial-rules-through-rage-myisha-cherry/ (accessed November 27, 2022).

20. Jaak Panksepp and Lucy Biven, *The Archaeology of Mind: Neuroevolutionary Origins of Human Emotions* (New York: W. W. Norton, 2012).

## CHAPTER 4

21. National Parks Service, "A Short History of Jamestown," US Department of the Interior, https://www.nps.gov/jame/learn/historyculture/a-short-history -of-jamestown.htm (accessed September 16, 2022).

22. See "privilege," in *Oxford Pocket Dictionary of Current English*, encyclope dia.com, https://www.encyclopedia.com/humanities/dictionaries-thesauruses -pictures-and-press-releases/privilege-0 (November 30, 2022).

23. Kendi, *Stamped from the Beginning*, 41.

24. Paul K. Piff, Daniel M. Stancato, Stéphane Côté, Rodolfo Mendoza-Denton, and Dacher Keltner, "Higher Social Class Predicts Increased Unethical Behavior," *Proceedings of the National Academy of Sciences* 109, no. 11 (2012): 4086–91, https://doi.org/10.1073/pnas.1118373109.

25. Michael W. Kraus and Dacher Keltner, "Social Class Rank, Essentialism, and Punitive Judgment," *Journal of Personality and Social Psychology* 105, no. 2 (2013): 247–61, https://doi.org/10.1037/a0032895.

26. Robin J. DiAngelo, *White Fragility: Why It's So Hard for White People to Talk about Racism* (Boston: Beacon Press, 2018).

## CHAPTER 5

27. Ryan Mac, "Facebook Apologizes after A.I. Puts 'Primates' Label on Video of Black Men," *New York Times*, September 3, 2021, https://www.nytimes .com/2021/09/03/technology/facebook-ai-race-primates.html. Kashmir Hill, "Wrongfully Accused by an Algorithm," *New York Times*, June 24, 2020, https:// www.nytimes.com/2020/06/24/technology/facial-recognition-arrest.html.

28. "Virginia Deputy Who Shot Black Man Appears to Mistake Phone for Gun," *The Guardian*, April 24, 2021, https://www.theguardian.com/us-news/2021/ apr/24/virginia-deputy-isaiah-brown-house-phone-gun. Cynthia Lee, "'But I Thought He Had a Gun'—Race and Police Use of Deadly Force," *Scholarly Commons*, George Washington University Law School, https://scholarship.law.gwu .edu/faculty_publications/785/ (accessed December 3, 2022). Joanna Slater and Lucia Walinchus, "He Was Killed by Police in His Bed. His Partner's Grief Has Just Begun," *Washington Post*, September 6, 2022, https://www.washingtonpost .com/nation/2022/09/05/ohio-shooting-donovan-lewis/.

29. "Study Shows Shoplifters More Readily Identified by Behavior, Not Race," *University of Florida News*, University of Florida, August 10, 2005, https://news.ufl .edu/archive/2005/08/study-shows-shoplifters-more-readily-identified-by-behav ior-not-race.html.

30. Jessica Nordell, *The End of Bias: A Beginning: The Science and Practice of Overcoming Unconscious Bias* (New York: Metropolitan Books, Henry Holt and Company, 2022), 272.

31. Jennifer L. Eberhardt, *Biased: Uncovering the Hidden Prejudice That Shapes What We See, Think, and Do* (London: Penguin Books, 2022).

32. Gordon Hodson and Kimberly Costello, "Interpersonal Disgust, Ideological Orientations, and Dehumanization as Predictors of Intergroup Attitudes," *Psychological Science* 18, no. 8 (2007): 691–98.

33. Sam Levin, "US Police Have Killed Nearly 600 People in Traffic Stops since 2017, Data Shows," *The Guardian,* April 21, 2022, https://www.theguardian.com/us-news/2022/apr/21/us-police-violence-traffic-stop-data.

## CHAPTER 6

34. Marshall B. Rosenberg, *Nonviolent Communication: A Language of Life,* 3rd edition (Encinitas, CA: PuddleDancer Press, 2015), 6.

## CHAPTER 7

35. Roxy Manning, *How to Have Antiracist Conversations: Embracing Our Full Humanity to Challenge White Supremacy* (Oakland, CA: Berrett-Koehler, 2023).

## CHAPTER 8

36. D. W. Sue, C. M. Capodilupo, G. C. Torino, J. M. Bucceri, A. M. B. Holder, K. L. Nadal, and M. Esquilin, "Racial Microaggressions in Everyday Life: Implications for Clinical Practice," *American Psychologist* 62, no. 4 (2007): 271–86, 271.

37. Isabel Wilkerson, *Caste: The Origins of Our Discontents* (New York: Random House, 2020).

38. All themes selected from Sue et al., "Racial Microaggressions in Everyday Life," 276–77.

39. E. Kate Webb, Claire M. Bird, Terri A. deRoon-Cassini, Carissa N. Weis, Ashley A. Huggins, Jacklynn M. Fitzgerald, Tara Miskovich et al., "Racial Discrimination and Resting-State Functional Connectivity of Salience Network Nodes in Trauma-Exposed Black Adults in the United States," *JAMA Network Open* 5, no. 1 (2022), https://doi.org/10.1001/jamanetworkopen.2021.44759.

40. L. B. Spanierman, D. A. Clark, and Y. Kim, "Reviewing Racial Microaggressions Research: Documenting Targets' Experiences, Harmful Sequelae, and Resistance Strategies," *Perspectives on Psychological Science* 16, no. 5 (2021): 1037–59.

41. X. P. Ding, G. Fu, and K. Lee, "Neural Correlates of Own- and Other-Race Face Recognition in Children: A Functional Near-Infrared Spectroscopy Study," *Neuroimage* 15, no. 85 (January 2014): 335–44, doi: 10.1016/j.neuroimage.2013.07.051, epub 2013 July 25, 2013, PMID: 23891903; PMCID: PMC3859716.

42. Arianna Bagnis, Alessia Celeghin, Matteo Diano, Carlos Andres Mendez, Giuliana Spadaro, Cristina Onesta Mosso, Alessio Avenanti, and Marco Tamietto, "Functional Neuroanatomy of Racial Categorization from Visual Perception: A Meta-Analytic Study," *NeuroImage* 217 (2020): 116939, https://doi.org/10.1016/j.neuroimage.2020.116939.

## CHAPTER 9

43. Stephen W. Porges, "Polyvagal Theory: A Biobehavioral Journey to Sociality," *Comprehensive Psychoneuroendocrinology* 7 (2021): 100069, https://doi.org/10.1016/j.cpnec.2021.100069.

44. Inbal Kashtan and Miki Kashtan, "Connection Requests: Motivations and Examples," in *BayNVC Nonviolent Communication Leadership Program* (Oakland, CA: BayNVC, 2014), 31–34.

## CHAPTER 10

45. Manny Diaz, "Florida Senate—2022 SB 148," Calendar for 11/27/2022—The Florida Senate, https://www.flsenate.gov/Session/Bill/2022/148/BillText/Filed/HTML (accessed November 27, 2022), lines 71–72.

46. Max Rollwage, Alisa Loosen, Tobias U. Hauser, Rani Moran, Raymond J. Dolan, and Stephen M. Fleming, "Confidence Drives a Neural Confirmation Bias," *Nature Communications* 11, no. 1 (2020), https://doi.org/10.1038/s41467-020-16278-6.

47. Caroline Davies, "Lady Hussey's Racist Remarks Will Take an Already Bruised Palace Two Steps Back," *The Guardian*, November 30, 2022, https://www.theguardian.com/uk-news/2022/nov/30/lady-husseys-racist-remarks-will-take-an-already-bruised-palace-two-steps-back.

48. Caroline Davies and Hannah Summers, "Prince William's Godmother Quits Palace over Comments to Black Charity Boss," *The Guardian*, November 30, 2022, https://www.theguardian.com/uk-news/2022/nov/30/buckingham-palace-aide-resigns-black-guest-traumatised-by-repeated-questioning.

## CHAPTER 11

49. Harvard Office for Equity, Diversity, Inclusion, and Belonging, "Calling In and Calling Out Guide," https://dib.harvard.edu/files/dib/files/calling_in_and_calling_out_guide_v4.pdf?m=1625683246 (accessed November 20, 2022).

50. Tufts Diversity and Inclusion, "Interrupting Bias: Calling Out vs. Calling In," Tufts University, February 10, 2021, https://diversity.tufts.edu/resources/interrupting-bias-calling-out-vs-calling-in/.

51. S. D. Glick, D. A. Ross, and L. B. Hough, "Lateral Asymmetry of Neurotransmitters in Human Brain," *Brain Research* 234, no. 1 (February 18, 1982): 53–63, doi: 10.1016/0006-8993(82)90472-3, PMID: 6120746.

## CONCLUSION

52. Library of Congress, *The Civil Rights Movement Knowledge Cards*, Pomegranate, 2003, https://www.pomegranate.com/products/the-civil-rights-movement-knowledge-cards.

53. Song Wang, Yajun Zhao, Jingguang Li, Han Lai, Chen Qiu, Nanfang Pan, and Qiyong Gong, "Neurostructural Correlates of Hope: Dispositional Hope Mediates the Impact of the SMA Gray Matter Volume on Subjective Well-Being in Late Adolescence," *Social Cognitive and Affective Neuroscience* 15, no. 4 (2020): 395–404, https://doi.org/10.1093/scan/nsaa046.

54. California State Parks, State of California, "About Coast Redwoods," https://www.parks.ca.gov/?page_id=22257 (accessed December 5, 2022).

55. Patricia G. Devine, Patrick S. Forscher, Anthony J. Austin, and William T. L. Cox, "Long-Term Reduction in Implicit Race Bias: A Prejudice Habit-Breaking Intervention," *Journal of Experimental Social Psychology* 48, no. 6 (2012): 1267–78, https://doi.org/10.1016/j.jesp.2012.06.003.

# ACKNOWLEDGMENTS

*From Sarah:*

Most important, I would like to thank Roxy Manning for being willing to take on this beautiful project with me in service of Beloved Community. I would also like to thank the following crew of readers, thinkers, and editors for their dedication to antiracism and self-compassion: Neal Maillet, Jeevan Sivasubramaniam, Elena Peyton-Jones, Jennifer Jones, James Peyton, Carol Ferris, Kamia Anderson-Harris, Nick Wood, Jaya Manske, Clare Crombie, Karen DeGannes, Jean McElhaney, Hannah Rubin, and most especially to Ranjana Ariaratnam and David Johnson.

*From Roxy:*

So many people supported this handbook and, in so doing, gifted me with healing. Thank you to:

Sarah Peyton—this handbook would not exist without your joy at the idea. Your rigor and delight when we nailed a concept, your capacity for relational efficiency and countless hours on video calls, co-writing, organizing, and just being present to help with the stuck places, your grace as we both navigate life-changing challenges.

Ranjana Ariaratnam, David Johnson, and Lakshmi Ariaratnam— who created and hosted my personal writer's retreat and provided unbelievable hours of eagle-eyed editing, conceptual holding, formatting wizardry, encouragement and laughter, dancing cats and scented-candle rituals, late-night accompaniment and gentle nudges.

Alejandra Delgado—for on-the-fly brainstorming, critical editing, and sharing relevant articles, for taking the load of both business and personal matters to free me to write, for meals and hanging with my family while I was busy, for laughter and shared vulnerability.

The Tower Team—Alejandra Delgado, Alicia Garcia, David Johnson, David Pursell, Donna Carter, Edmundo Norte, Janey Skinner, Kristin Masters, Mike Tinoco, Ranjana Ariaratnam, Shannon Casey, Susan Strasburger, Talli Jackson—who insisted I remember that I'm part of a village and showed up to read chapters, offer their knowledge in all the topics of this handbook, brainstorm on long video calls, share their experiences and volunteer in dialogues, and provide edits and suggestions.

Mireille van Bremen—for illustrations emerging from generous listening that captured the heart of the work, for precision, for mourning together and celebrations. I smile each time I look at the "Needs and Values" chart!

Our editor, Neal Maillet—who took a chance on an unknown author, ran with our unconventional strategy to get this handbook on Berrett-Koehler's catalog and made my dream possible! The BK staff, who greenlighted this project and responded with grace and enthusiasm to share their expertise and make this work better. And David Peattie and the amazing folks at BookMatters, especially Amy Smith Bell, who demonstrated how much better, in clarity and content, copyediting can make a book!

Our Kickstarter backers—who jumped in when we asked for evidence that these books were wanted in the world.

And my family: My dad, Milton Manning, who read many books on history with me when I was small and did not get to see this handbook; my mom, Lois Manning, who read chapters and joined calls, beaming with pride, who cooked my favorite meals to lift my spirits and believed "anything is possible." My children: Anika—for meals and banana bread, bumblebees, octopi, jellyfish, and trips to the store; Theo—for curiosity and laughter and modeling perseverance; and Micah—who would have been so delighted to hold this handbook in his hands.

# INDEX

Page numbers with *f* refer to figures.

**ROXY MANNING**, PhD (*right*), clinical psychologist and Certified Trainer of Nonviolent Communication, brings decades of service experience to her work interrupting explicitly and implicitly oppressive attitudes and cultural norms. Roxy has worked, consulted, and provided training across the United States with businesses, nonprofits, and government organizations wanting to move toward equitable and diverse workplace cultures, as well as internationally in more than ten countries with individuals and groups committed to social justice. As a psychologist, she works in San Francisco serving the homeless and disenfranchised mentally ill population. Roxy is also the author of *How to Have Antiracist Conversations: Embracing Our Full Humanity to Challenge White Supremacy.*

**SARAH PEYTON** (*left*), Certified Trainer of Nonviolent Communication and neuroscience educator, integrates brain science and the use of resonant language to awaken and sustain self-compassion, particularly in the face of such difficult issues as self-condemnation, self-disgust, and self-sabotage. She teaches and lectures internationally and is the author of the *Your Resonant Self* book series.

# Berrett–Koehler
## Publishers

**Berrett-Koehler** is an independent publisher dedicated to an ambitious mission: *Connecting people and ideas to create a world that works for all.*

Our publications span many formats, including print, digital, audio, and video. We also offer online resources, training, and gatherings. And we will continue expanding our products and services to advance our mission.

We believe that the solutions to the world's problems will come from all of us, working at all levels: in our society, in our organizations, and in our own lives. Our publications and resources offer pathways to creating a more just, equitable, and sustainable society. They help people make their organizations more humane, democratic, diverse, and effective (and we don't think there's any contradiction there). And they guide people in creating positive change in their own lives and aligning their personal practices with their aspirations for a better world.

And we strive to practice what we preach through what we call "The BK Way." At the core of this approach is *stewardship,* a deep sense of responsibility to administer the company for the benefit of all of our stakeholder groups, including authors, customers, employees, investors, service providers, sales partners, and the communities and environment around us. Everything we do is built around stewardship and our other core values of *quality, partnership, inclusion,* and *sustainability.*

This is why Berrett-Koehler is the first book publishing company to be both a B Corporation (a rigorous certification) and a benefit corporation (a for-profit legal status), which together require us to adhere to the highest standards for corporate, social, and environmental performance. And it is why we have instituted many pioneering practices (which you can learn about at www.bkconnection.com), including the Berrett-Koehler Constitution, the Bill of Rights and Responsibilities for BK Authors, and our unique Author Days.

We are grateful to our readers, authors, and other friends who are supporting our mission. We ask you to share with us examples of how BK publications and resources are making a difference in your lives, organizations, and communities at www.bkconnection.com/impact.

Dear reader,

Thank you for picking up this book and welcome to the worldwide BK community! You're joining a special group of people who have come together to create positive change in their lives, organizations, and communities.

## What's BK all about?

Our mission is to connect people and ideas to create a world that works for all.

Why? Our communities, organizations, and lives get bogged down by old paradigms of self-interest, exclusion, hierarchy, and privilege. But we believe that can change. That's why we seek the leading experts on these challenges—and share their actionable ideas with you.

## A welcome gift

To help you get started, we'd like to offer you a **free copy** of one of our bestselling ebooks:

### www.bkconnection.com/welcome

When you claim your **free ebook**, you'll also be subscribed to our blog.

## Our freshest insights

Access the best new tools and ideas for leaders at all levels on our blog at ideas.bkconnection.com.

Sincerely,

Your friends at Berrett-Koehler

Certified

Corporation